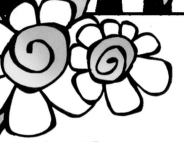

So This is Me

So this is me...I'm a tad wacky and just shy of crazy.

And I love to create. Whether I'm painting fine art in my studio, drawing my wacky characters on location at shows, sitting at my pottery wheel on my back porch, or writing at my computer, the creative process is liberating beyond words. I am forever exploring new ways to express the energy inside me. But I feel forever blessed to have these gifts and vow to never take them for granted.

I'm 50-something years old and live mere feet from the ocean in a funky little surf town called New Smyrna Beach, Florida. Yes, I know. New Smyrna Beach has been officially declared the "Shark Bite Capital of the World," but the sand sparkles like white crystals and the water is a thousand shades of aqua blue. Waking up every morning to this glorious sight makes my heart tingle. I share that space with my husband, Al, and a goofy Labrador retriever named Lucy. I eat chocolate truffles while I paint—and when they run out, I quit. I drink Perrier sparkling water so often I'm considering taking out stock in the company. I practice yoga, which for some strange reason I think will help compensate for my horrible diet, and I sit on the beach with my toes in the sand every chance I get.

I have five grown children and fourteen grandkids who love me as much as I adore them. I've taught them to dip their French fries in their chocolate shakes, make up any words they want to any tune they like, and to never, ever color inside the lines. (However, they all feel the need to assure their friends that they also have another set of grandparents who are "normal.")

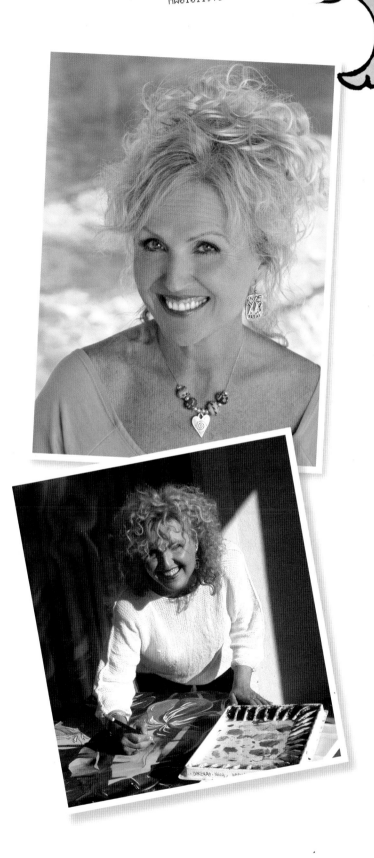

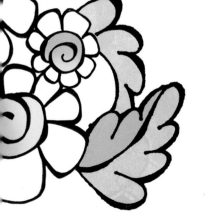

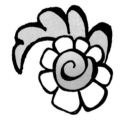

Here are some examples of my wacky characters and other work that I have painted with my favorite medium, watercolors.

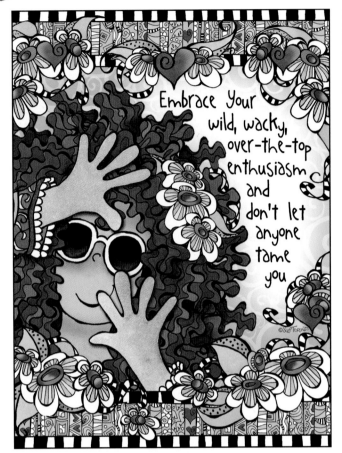

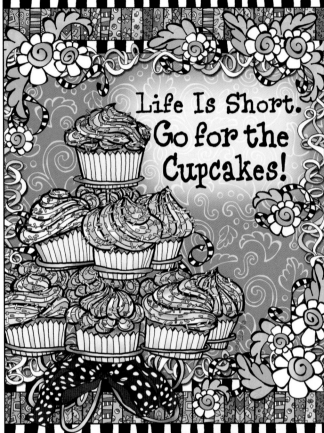

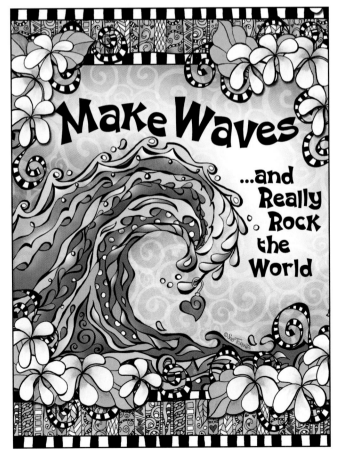

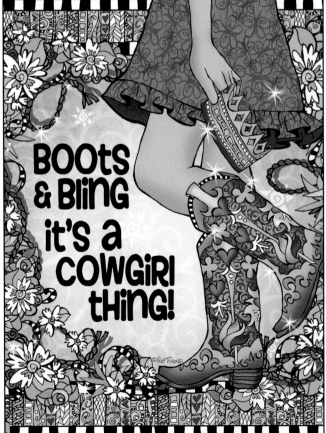

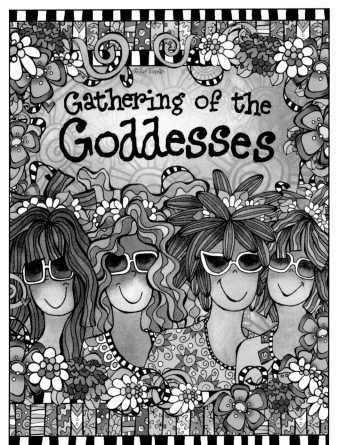

Gathering of the Goddesses

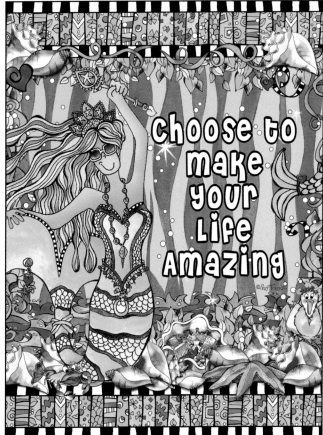

choose to make your life Amazing

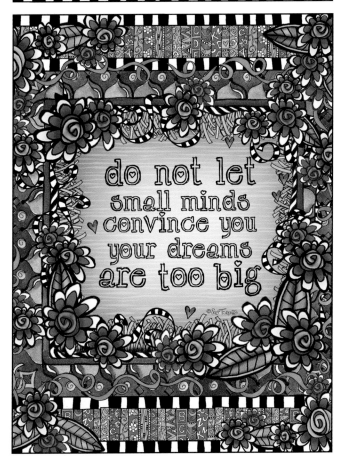

do not let small minds convince you your dreams are too big

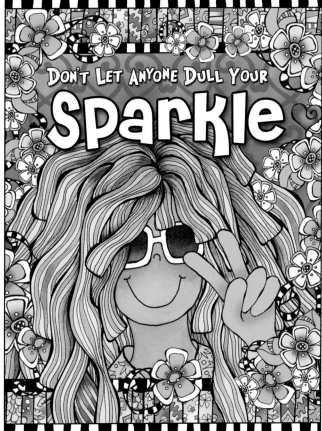

DON'T LET ANYONE DULL YOUR SparKle

Add the Color...
Feel the Tingle

There's nothing more satisfying than finishing a work of art. It adds excitement and joy to your life. Or to use my favorite tag line, you "Feel the Tingle."

The fact is, not everyone likes to draw, but everybody loves to color. Thus, anyone can experience the joy of participating in creating a piece of art with a coloring book. That's the genius of the medium. It's fun, interesting, and very fulfilling.

It doesn't matter how creative you are, you can learn about color and finish a masterpiece worth displaying. That's the purpose of this introduction—to teach you this skill.

If you already know this stuff, have a ball. If you don't, this information is way worth the effort. It will influence the way you color your entire world, from your home to your clothing to your food. Yes, even how you apply your makeup. And you will become a coloring book guru to boot.

So let's begin.

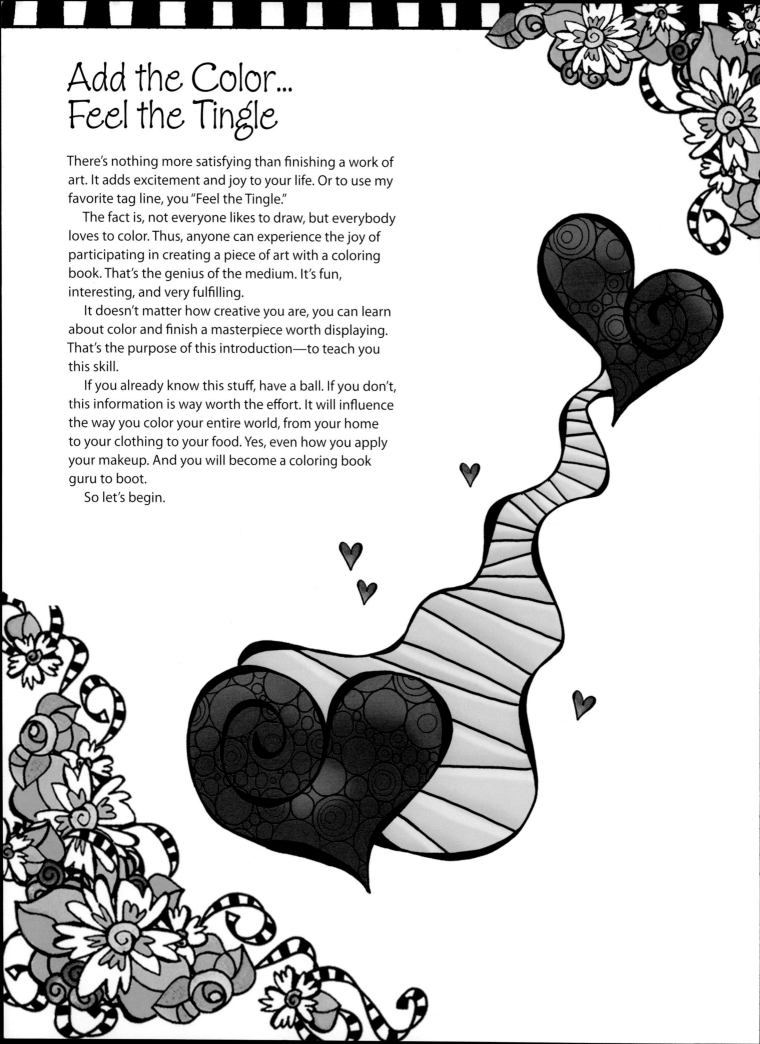

Color Selection Is Critical

You definitely want that "wow" factor when you're finished. So you need to know which colors do and do not complement each other. Do it right, and it will look like a Picasso.

The most essential tool in color selection is the color wheel, presented to the right. Each color in the wheel is either PRIMARY, SECONDARY, or TERTIARY.

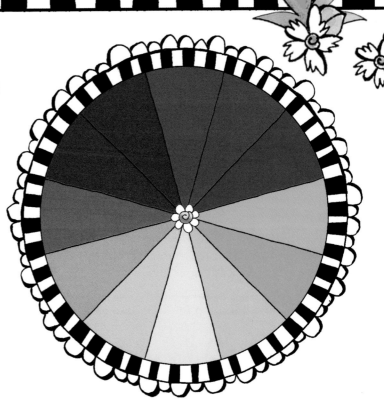

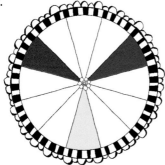

The primary colors are red, yellow, and blue. These are the root colors—they can't be created by mixing other colors. They are the pure foundation of the color wheel. All other colors are some combination of these three.

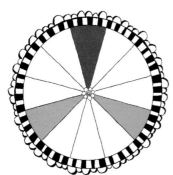

The secondary colors are orange, green, and purple. They are simply an equal mix of two primary colors (red + yellow = orange, yellow + blue = green, and blue + red = purple).

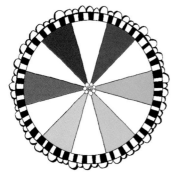

Tertiary colors are created by mixing a primary color with a secondary color. The resulting color is a matter of the percentage of the colors in the mix. There is no end to tertiary colors.

Colors are also categorized as warm or cool. Red, yellow, and orange are warm colors. Green, blue, and purple are cool colors. Selecting warm or cool colors really sets the mood of your piece. Warm colors are bold and exciting, while cool colors are more calm and peaceful.

Things really get interesting when you start playing with variations of a color. You can "tint" a color by adding white to the mix. Or you can "shade" a color by adding black.

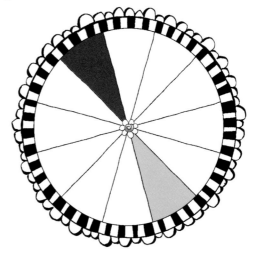

Colors opposite each other on the color wheel are called "complementary" and really pop off the page when they are used adjacent to each other. That's why you see yellow writing on purple backgrounds on billboards all over town. Or vice versa.

My Personal Twist

Since my earliest days as an artist, I have embraced the color yellow. Whether I am painting in my preferred medium of watercolors or dabbling in acrylics, pencils, markers, inks, or crayons, I almost always start with a layer of pale yellow—especially on a piece I want to be on the warm side of the color wheel. This assures that any work of art gets a wash of sunshine, whether the final colors are green, yellow, orange, or red. It really makes the colors pop. Greens get limey, oranges get a tangerine glow, reds get fiery, and yellows get even more electric.

And don't forget to leave open spaces with no color for white. It's easy to want to color every single nook and cranny with one of your fun colors, but leaving enough white is just as important to give your finished piece a lovely balance.

This is how I add a unique touch that is totally me. You should experiment with your own ways to make the art feel uniquely you! You might do this with your color choices or by adding patterns and flourishes to the art (check out the open spaces at the top and bottom of each piece, perfect for patterning). Have fun playing around!

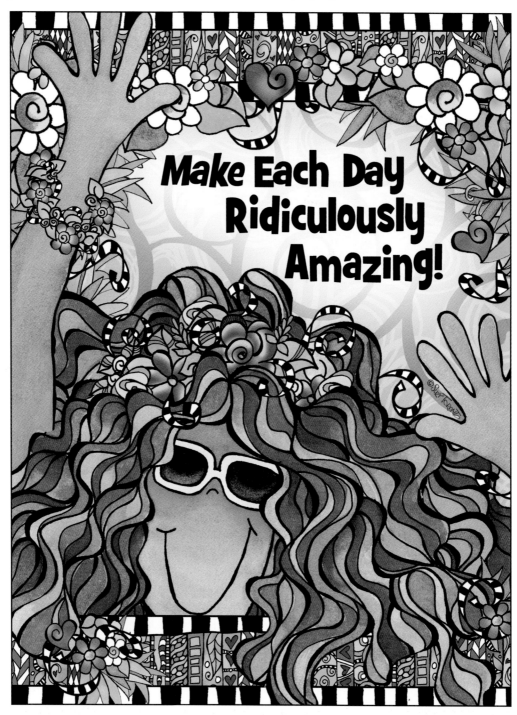

Make Each Day Ridiculously Amazing!

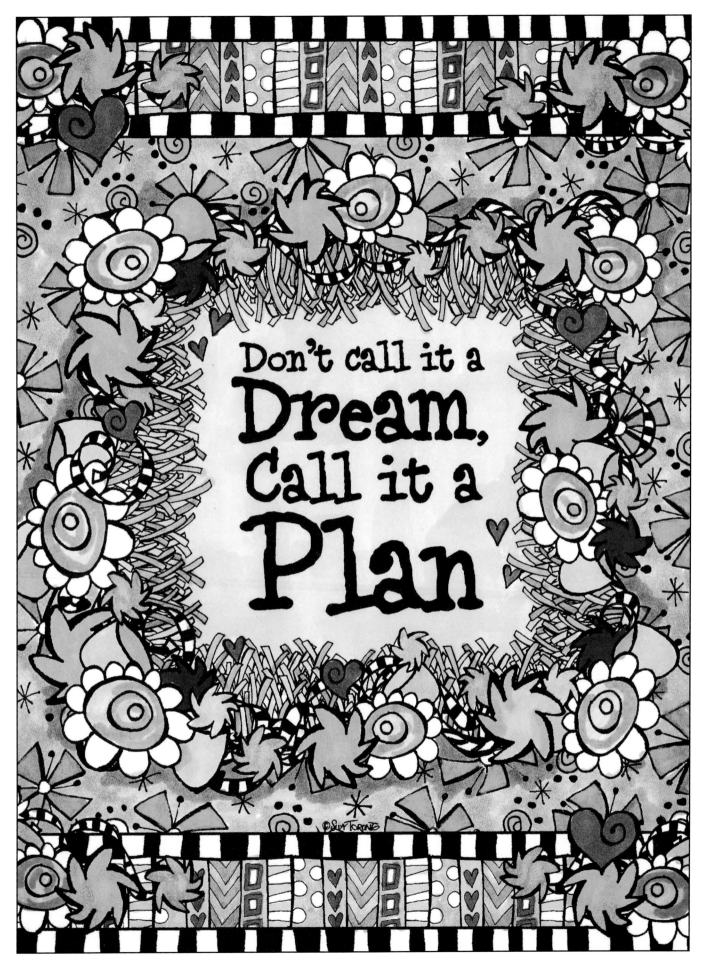

Don't call it a
Dream,
Call it a
Plan

Call It a Plan, Color by Erica Avedikian

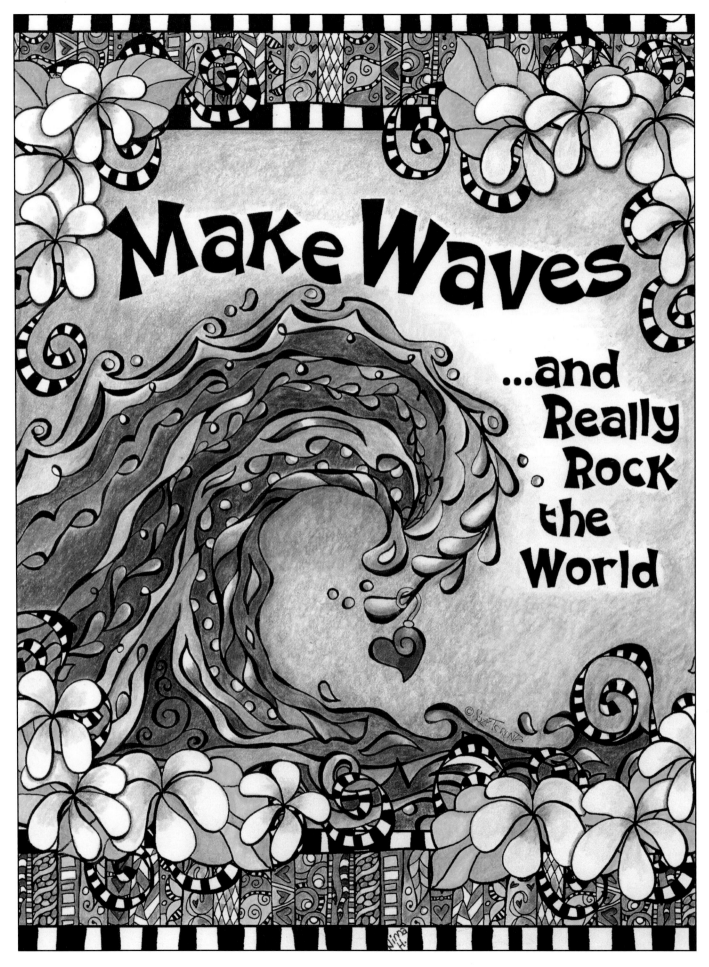

Make Waves

...and Really Rock the World

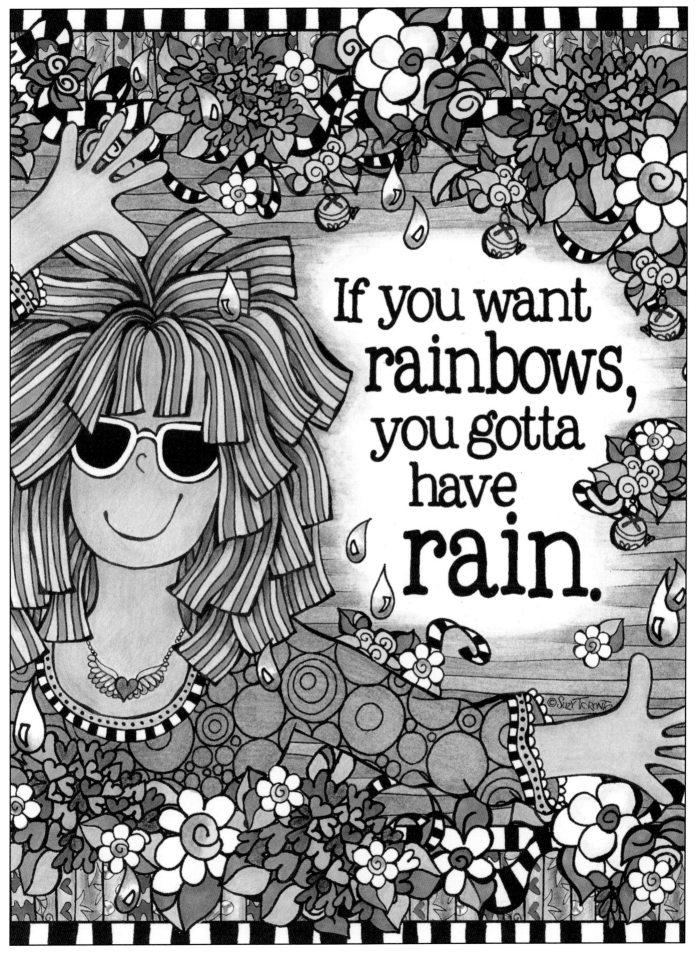

If you want rainbows, you gotta have rain.

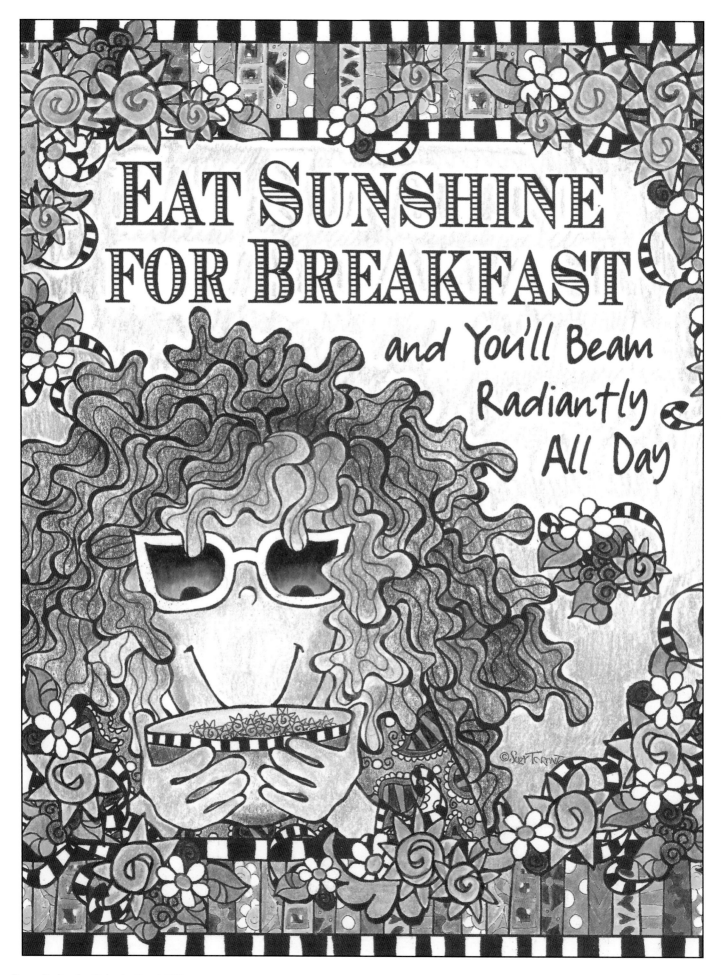

Beam Radiantly, Color by Sarah Wilson

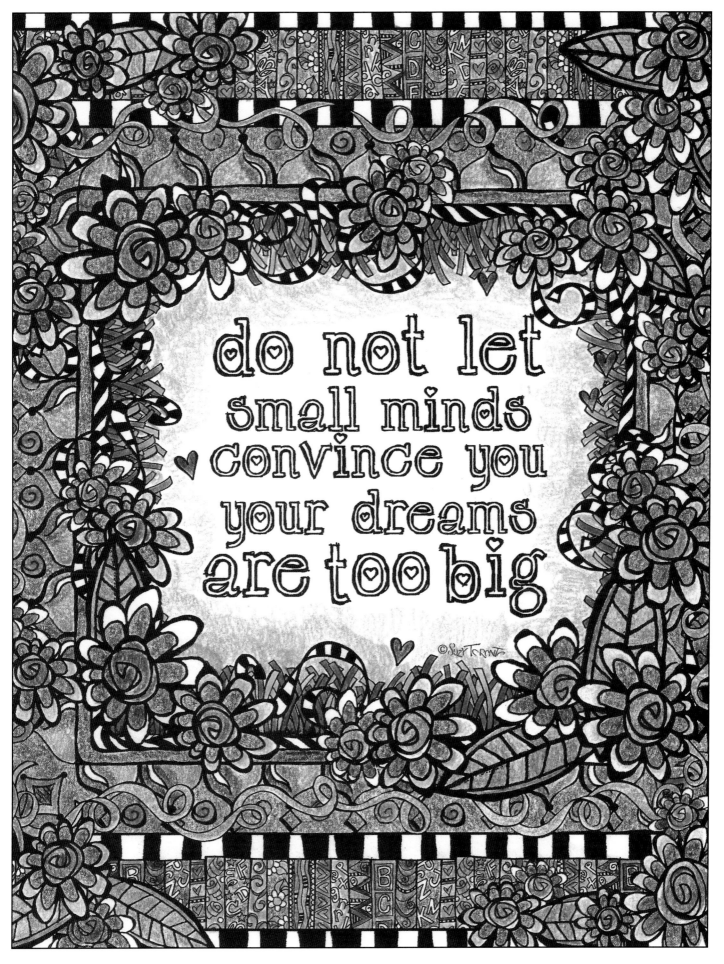

do not let small minds convince you your dreams are too big

Small Minds, Color by Sarah Wilson

©Suzy Toronto • suzytoronto.com • From *Inspiration & Encouragement Coloring Book* ©Design Originals, www.D-Originals.com

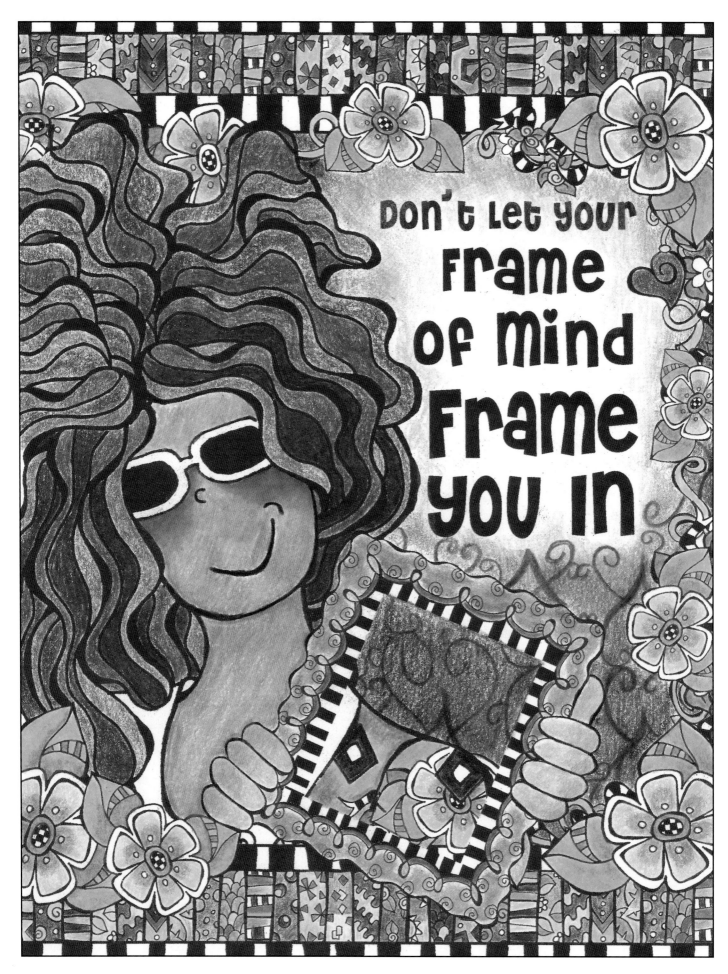

Don't Let your Frame of Mind Frame you in

Your Frame of Mind, Color by Sarah Wilson

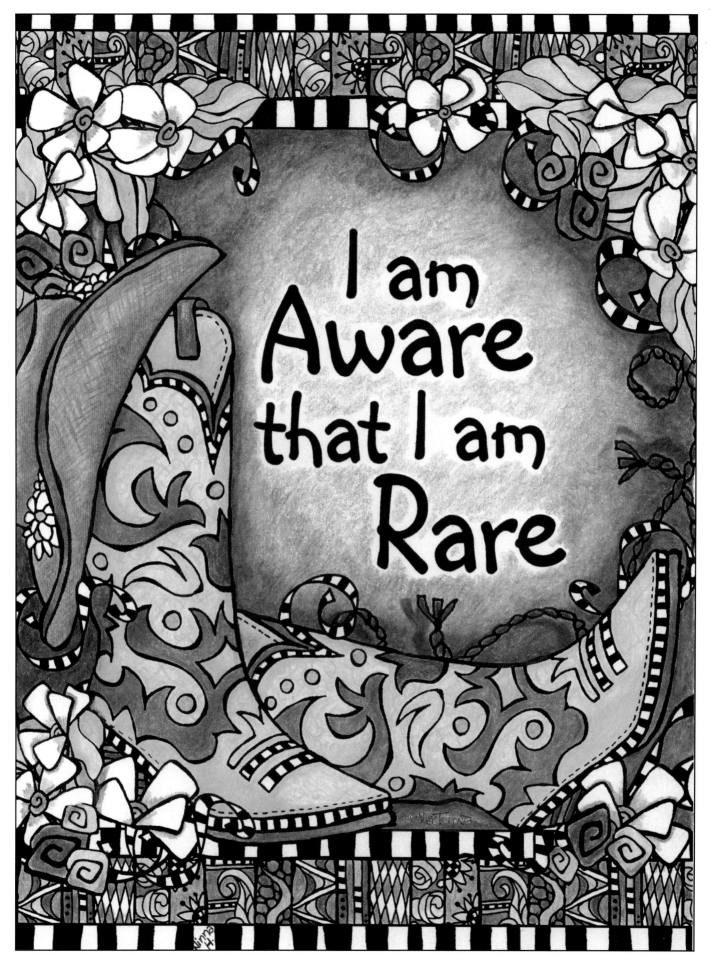

I am Aware that I am Rare

I Am Rare, Color by Ninna Hellman

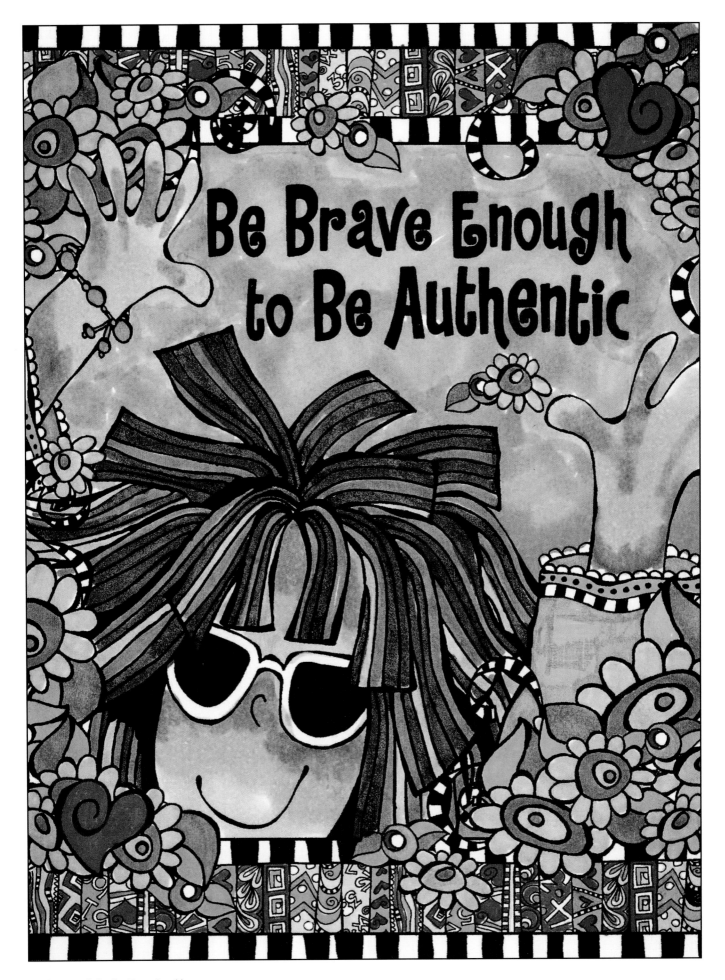

Be Authentic, Color by Erica Avedikian

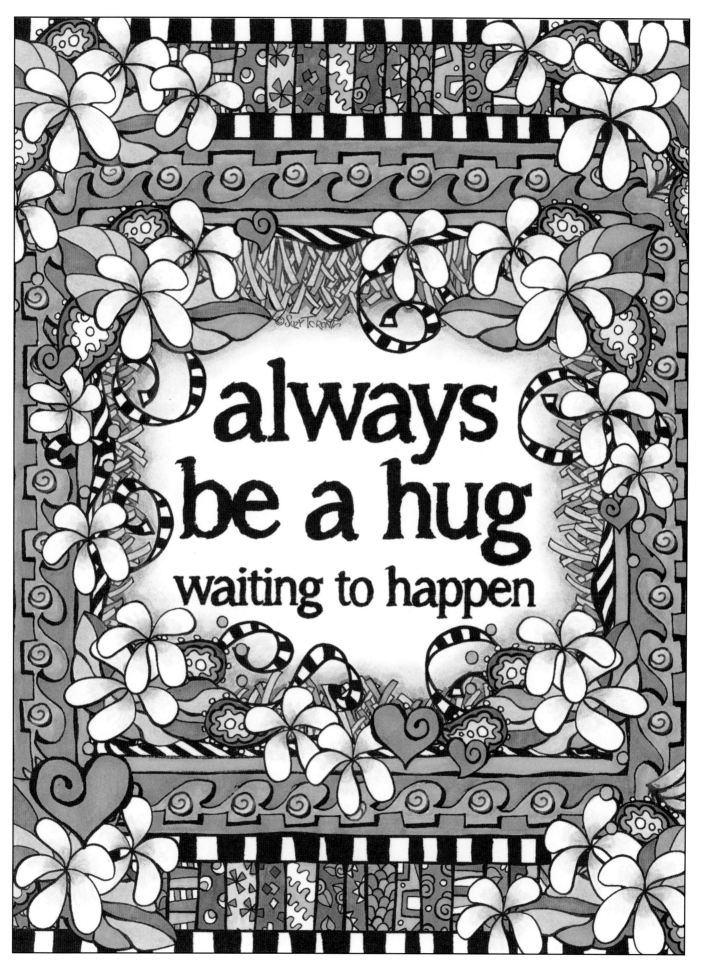

always be a hug
waiting to happen

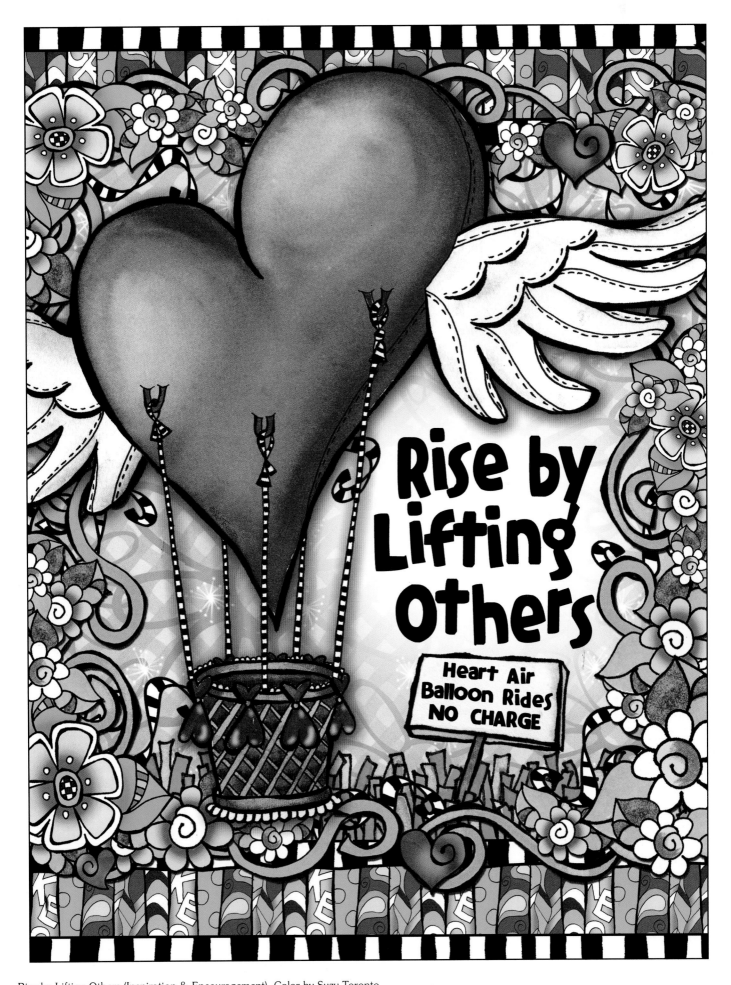

Rise by Lifting Others (Inspiration & Encouragement), Color by Suzy Toronto

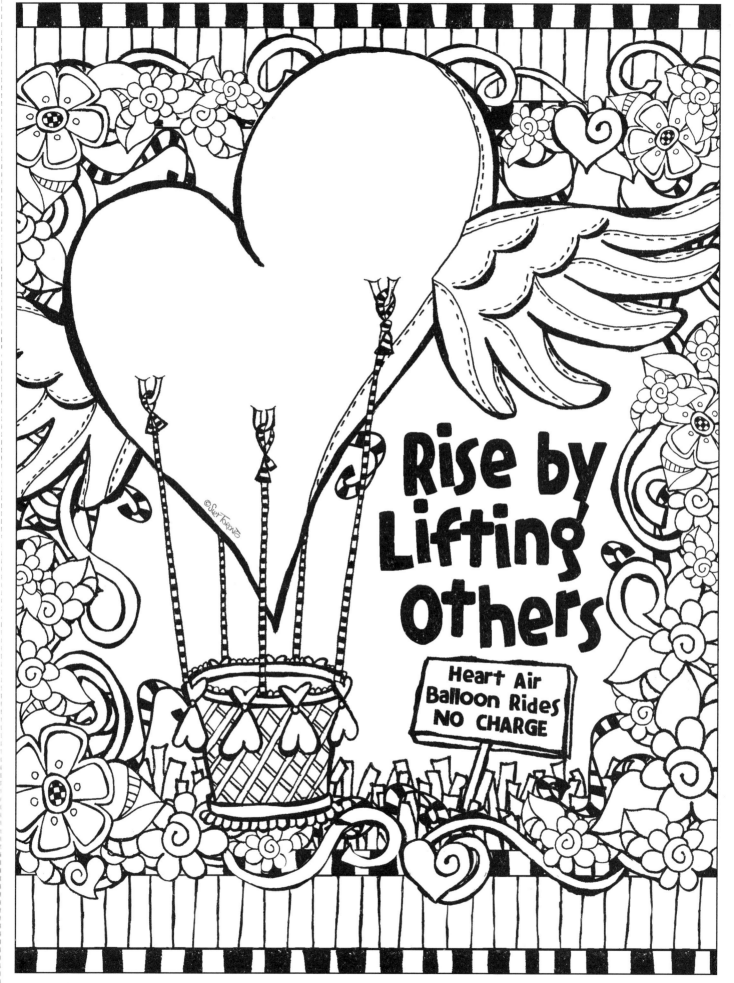

Rise by Lifting Others

Heart Air
Balloon Rides
NO CHARGE

If you're too busy to serve others,
you're simply too busy.

Rise by Lifting Others (Inspiration & Encouragement)

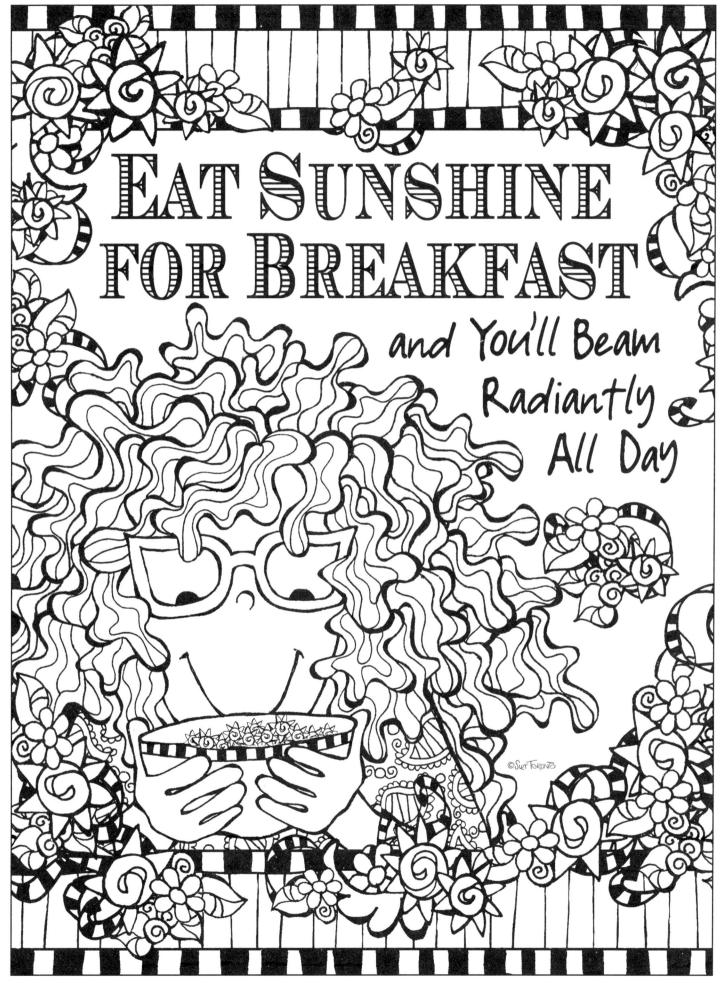

When you let your light shine from
within, you give others permission
to do the same.

_____
_____
_____
_____
_____
_____
_____
_____

Beam Radiantly

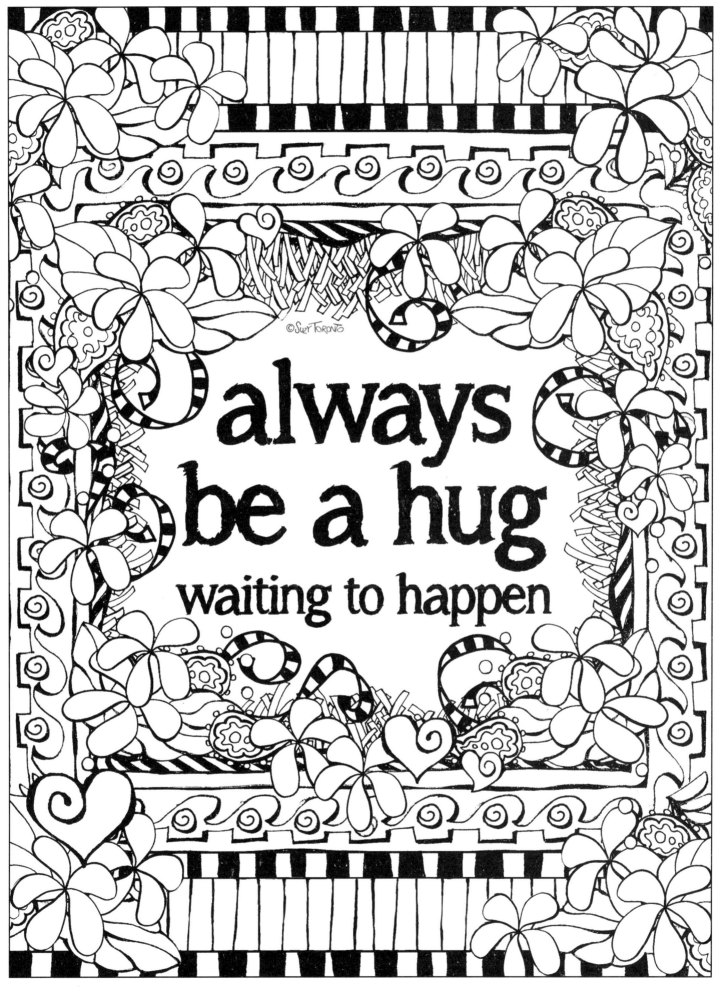

always be a hug waiting to happen

Never put off until tomorrow
what you can hug today.

A Hug Waiting to Happen

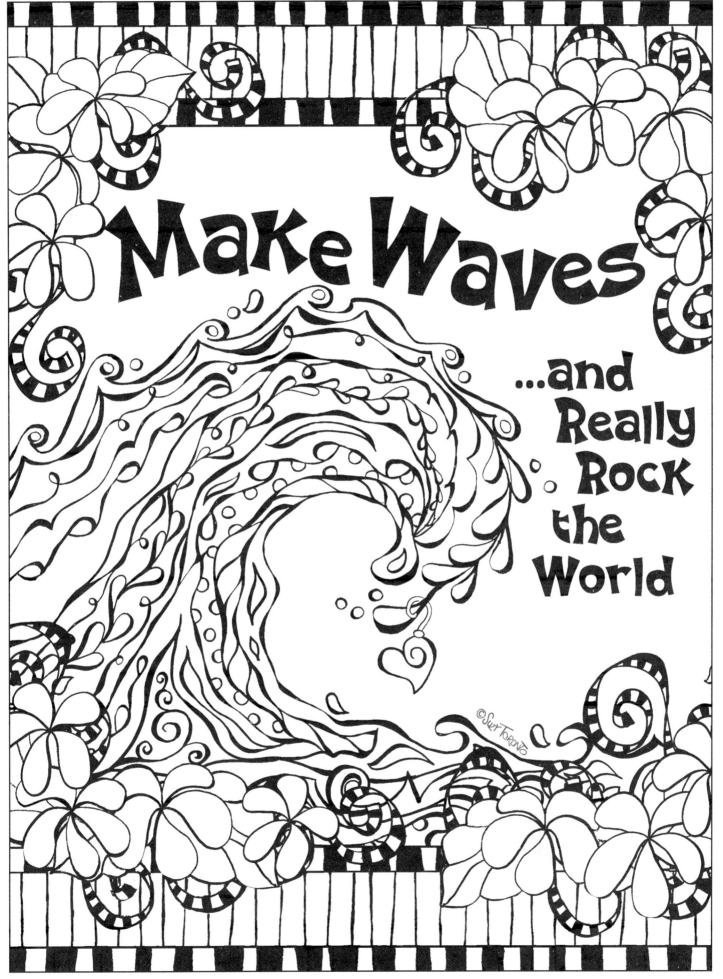

People who are crazy enough to think
they can make a difference in the
world are the ones who actually do.

_____
_____
_____
_____
_____
_____
_____
_____

Make Waves

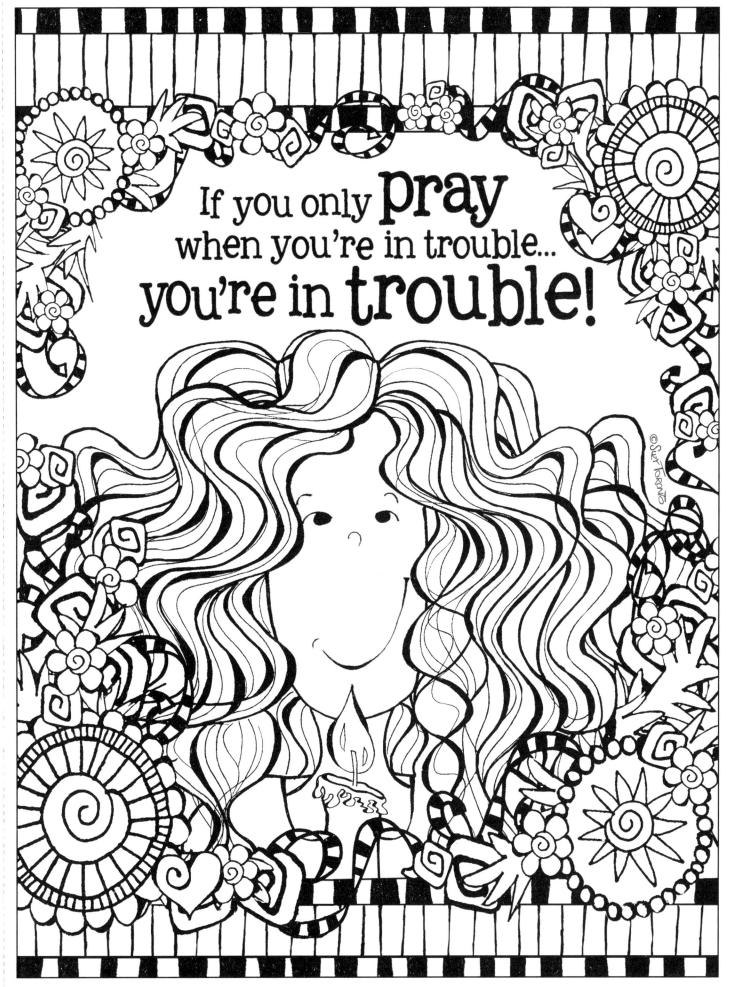

If you only **pray**
when you're in trouble...
you're in trouble!

©Suz Toronto

Don't be afraid to let someone
see you pray.

_____
_____
_____
_____
_____
_____
_____
_____
_____
_____
_____

Pray

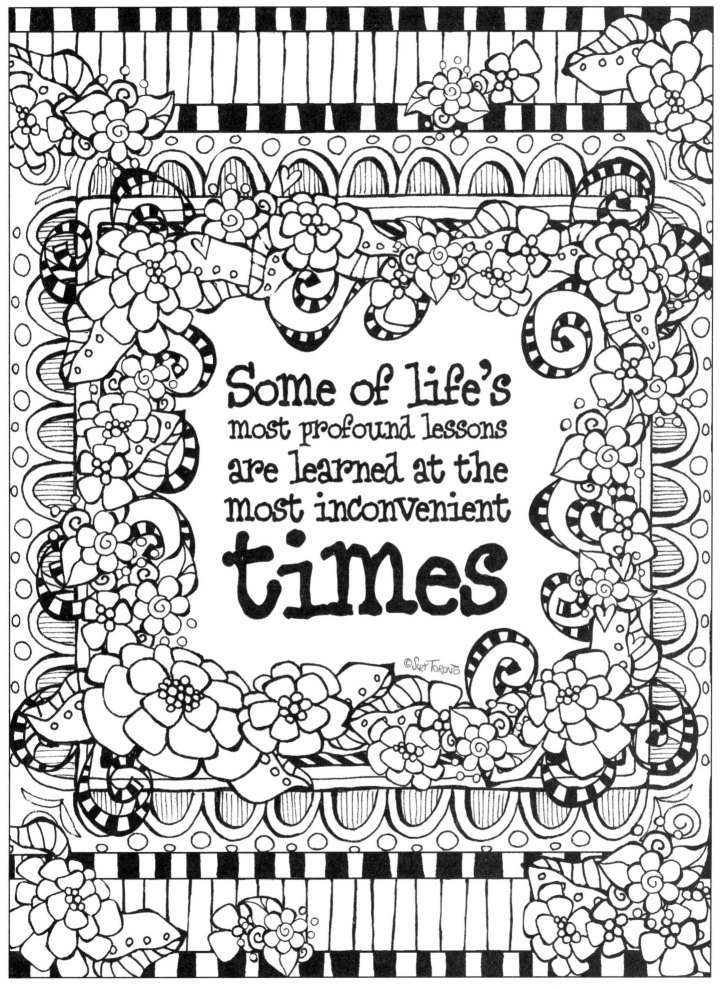

Some of life's most profound lessons are learned at the most inconvenient times

©Suzy Toronto

Face your challenges head on—with
grace, style, and conviction.

_____
_____
_____
_____
_____
_____
_____
_____

Life's Lessons

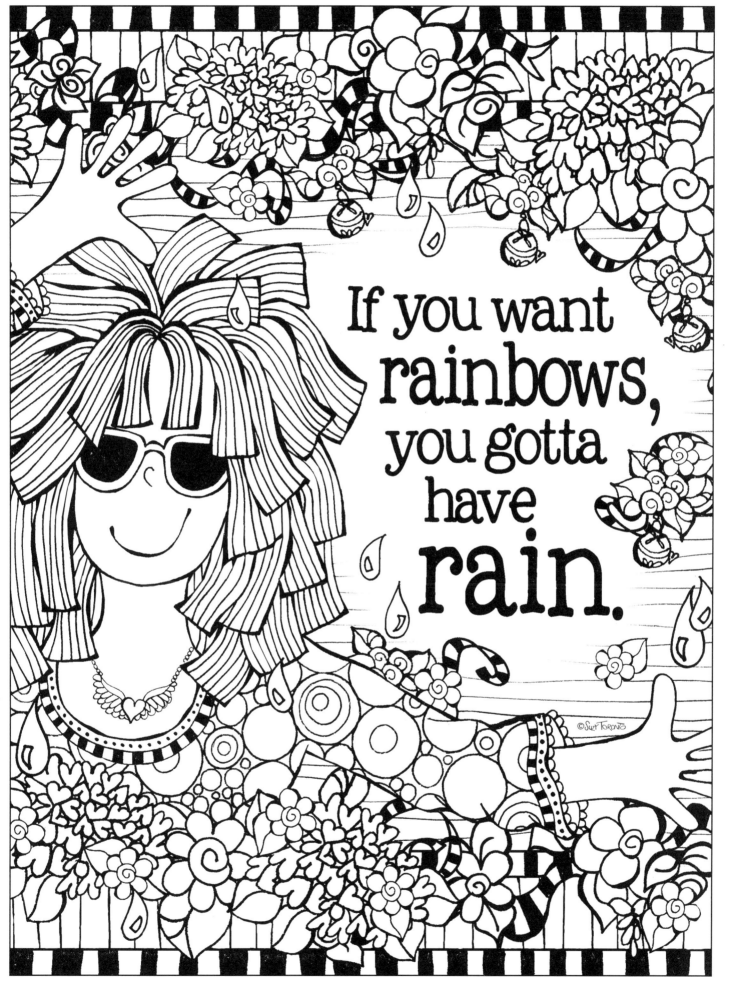

If you want rainbows, you gotta have rain.

You never realize how high you are
without knowing how low you've been.

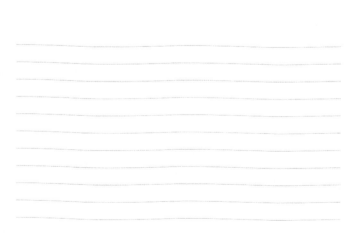

Rainbows

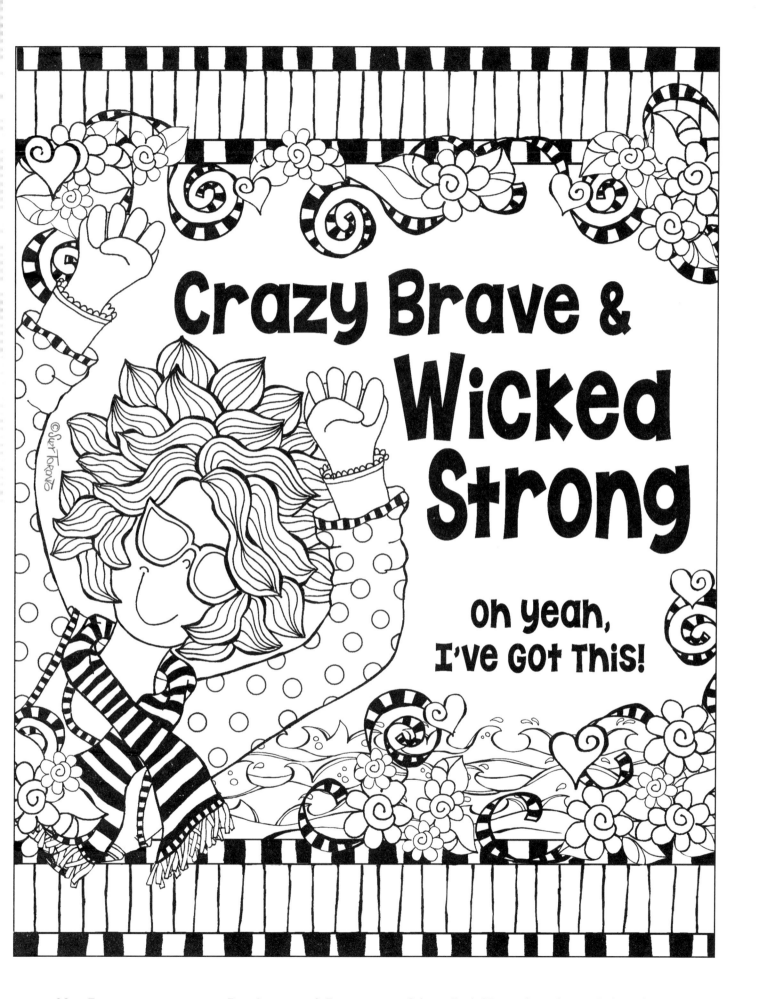

Crazy Brave &
Wicked
Strong

oh yeah,
I've Got This!

The potential is within you to be and
do anything you set your mind to.

_____
_____
_____
_____
_____
_____
_____
_____
_____

Crazy Brave & Wicked Strong
(Inspiration & Encouragement)

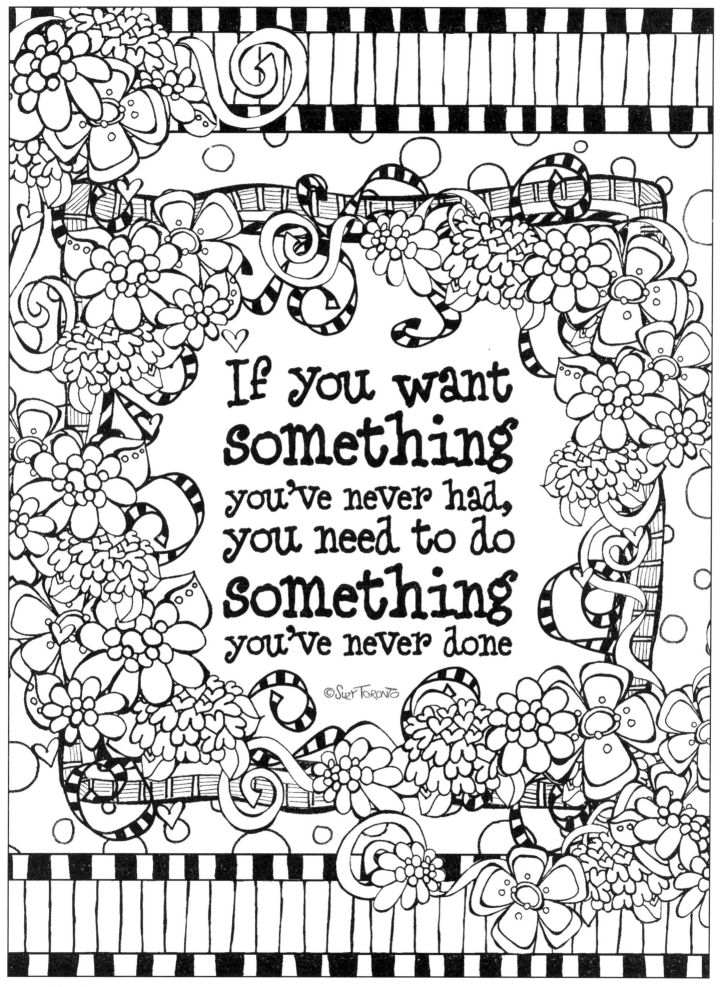

If you want something you've never had, you need to do something you've never done

©Suzy Toronto

Something wonderful is out there
waiting to happen, and it's got
your name all over it.

_____
_____
_____
_____
_____
_____
_____
_____
_____

Do Something You've Never Done

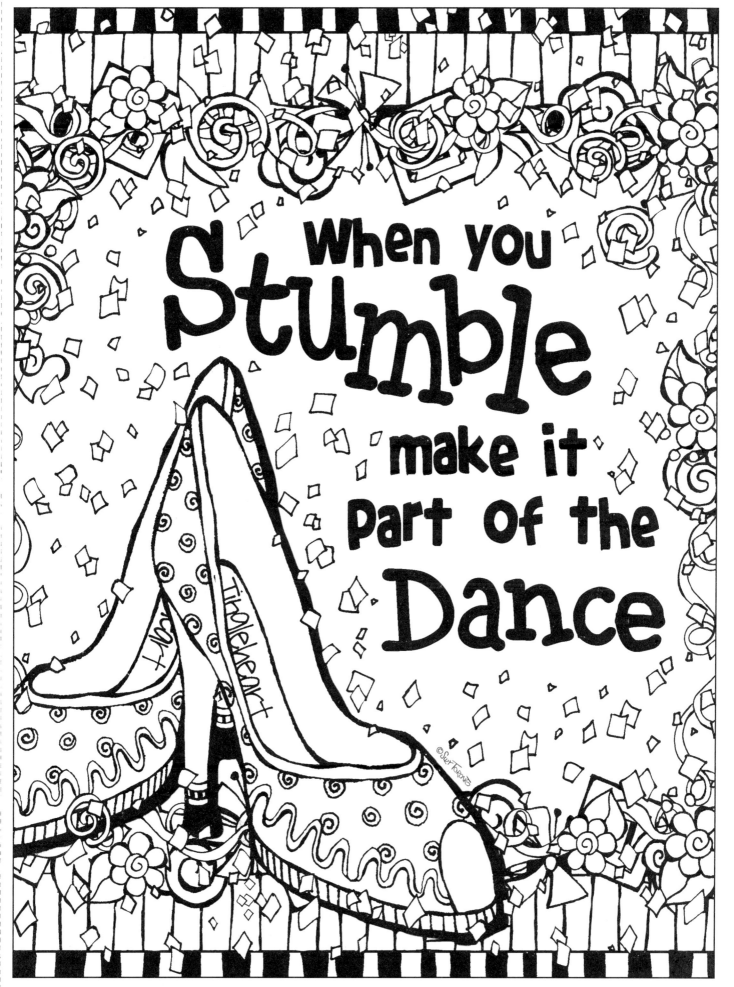

When you **Stumble** make it part of the **Dance**

There IS a "Do-Over" button.
It's labeled "Keep Trying."

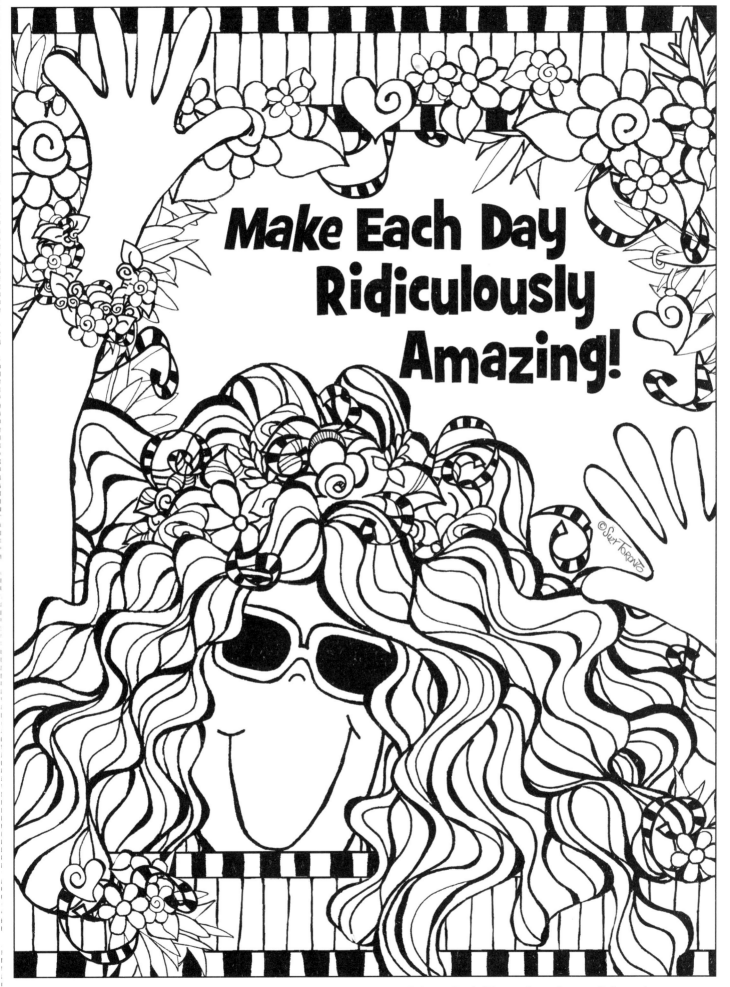

Make Each Day Ridiculously Amazing!

Be willing to step outside the box,
throw caution to the wind, and grab
hold of the shiny brass ring. (I happen
to know it has your name on it!)

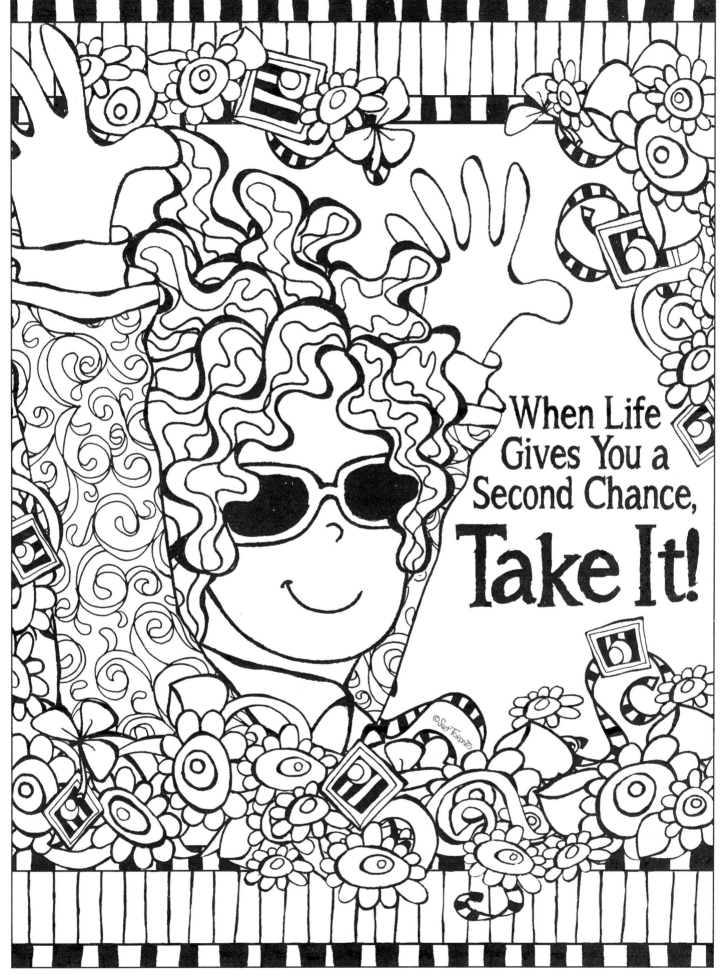

When Life Gives You a Second Chance, **Take It!**

Stop what you're doing and start living.

Second Chance

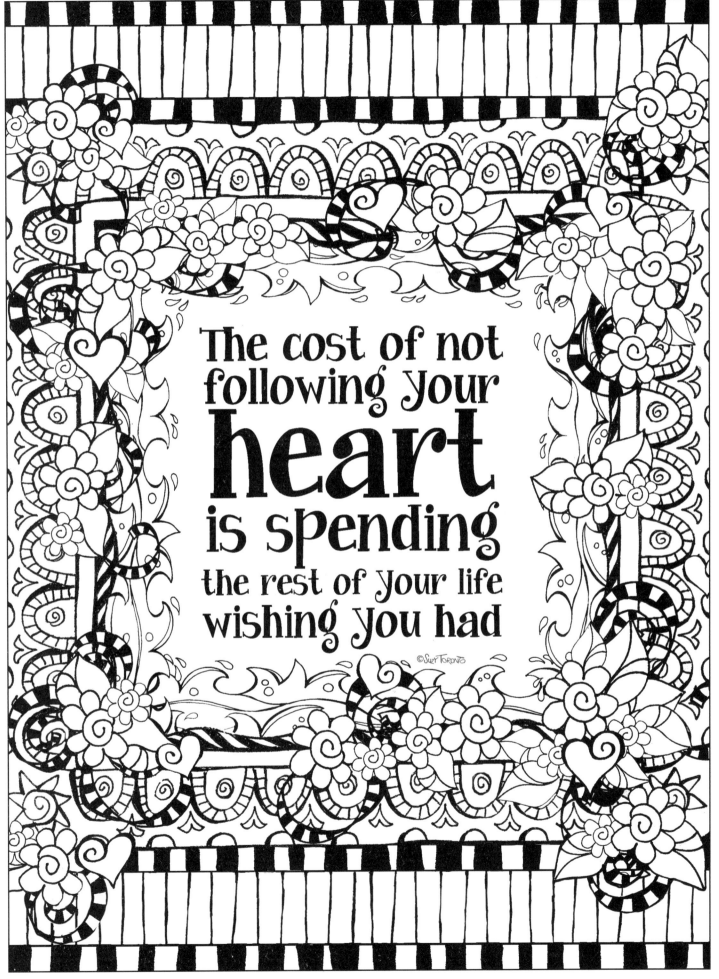

The cost of not following your **heart** is spending the rest of your life wishing you had

©Suzy Toronto

Change is always scary but the
alternative is living with regret.

_____
_____
_____
_____
_____
_____
_____
_____
_____
_____

Follow Your Heart

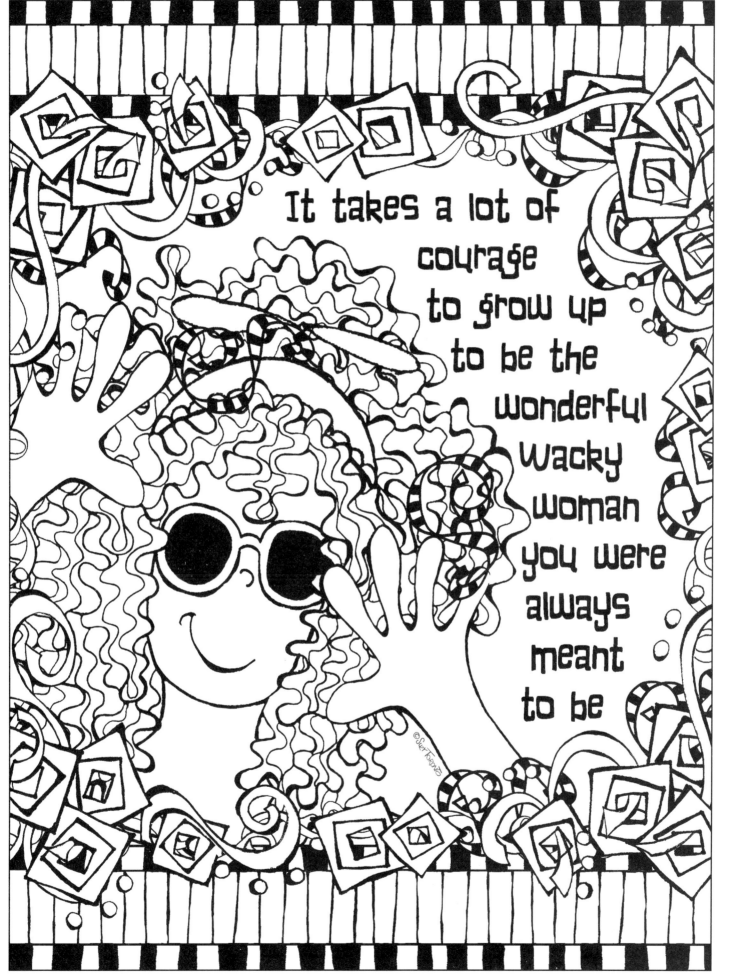

It takes a lot of courage to grow up to be the wonderful wacky woman you were always meant to be

Don't forget to be awesome.

The Courage to Grow Up

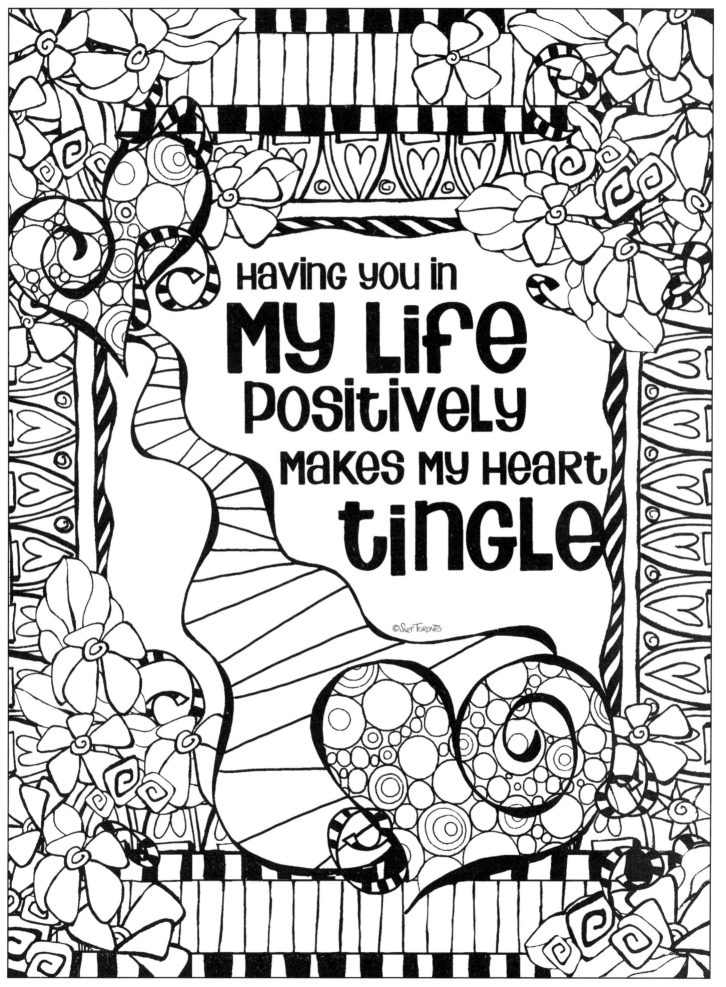

Having you in
MY LIFE
Positively
makes my heart
tingle

©Suzy Toronto

I can't imagine getting through a day,
much less eternity, without you.

_____
_____
_____
_____
_____
_____
_____
_____
_____

You Make My Heart Tingle

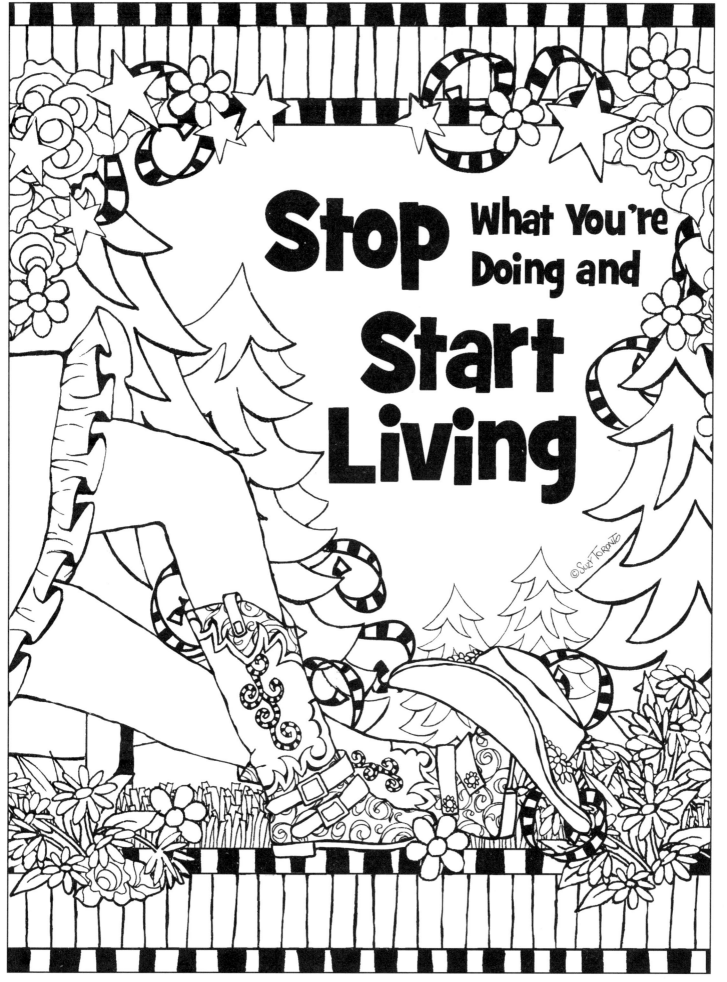

Life is short. What are you waiting for?
It's time to take that leap of faith.
Just believe.

_____
_____
_____
_____
_____
_____
_____
_____
_____
_____

Start Living

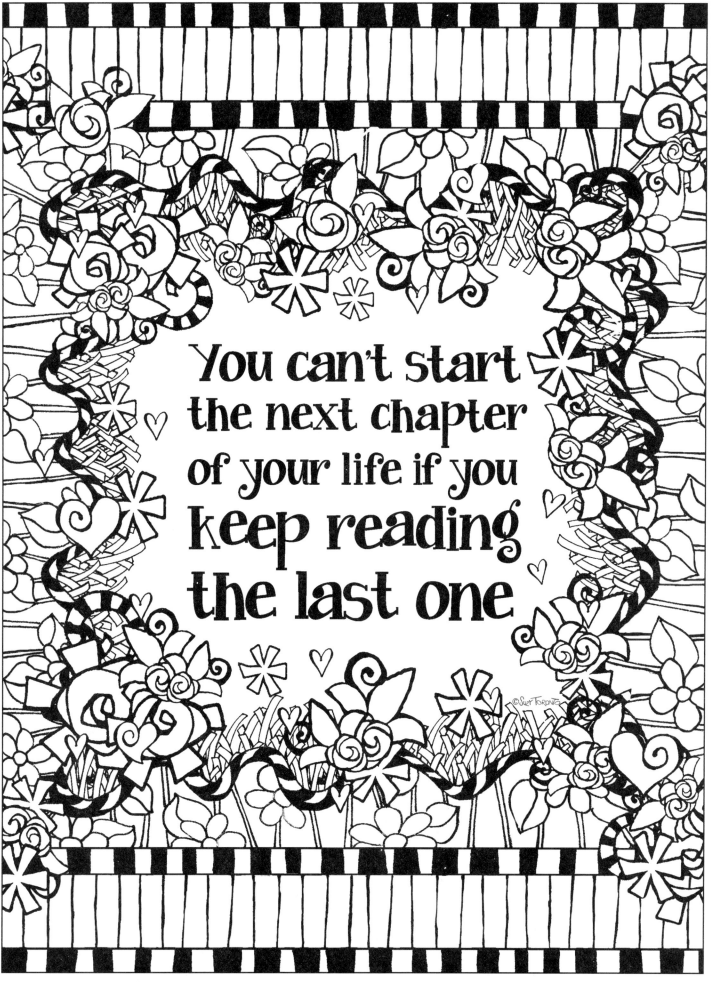

You can't start the next chapter of your life if you keep reading the last one

If you change nothing,
nothing will change.

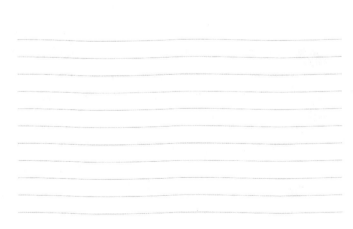

Start the Next Chapter

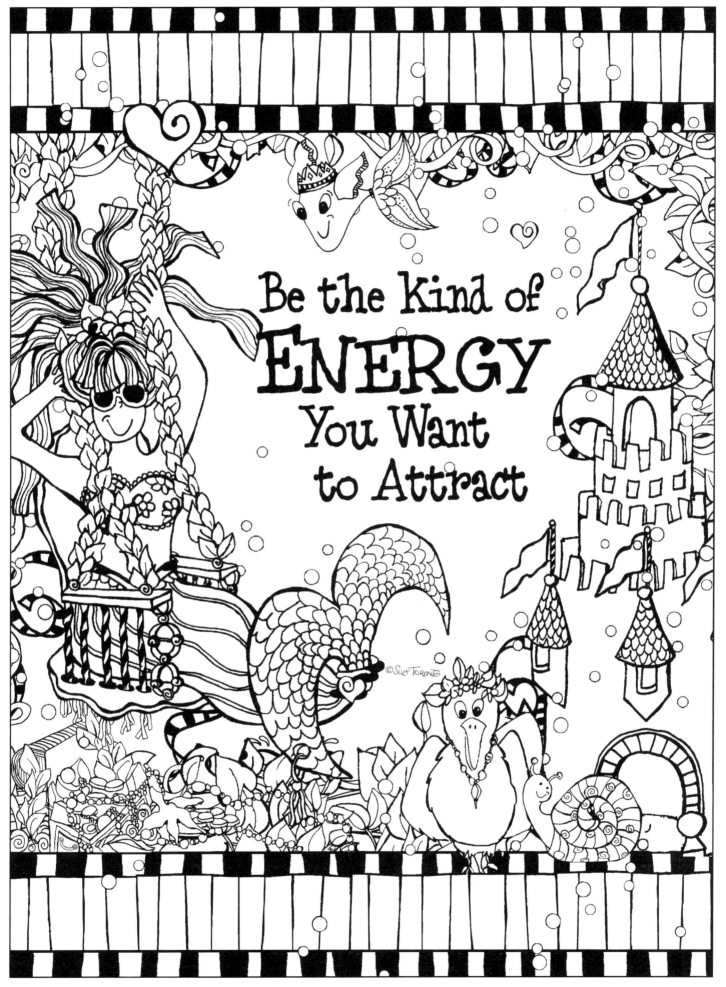

Be the Kind of **ENERGY** You Want to Attract

We possess within us the
potential to light up the world.

_____
_____
_____
_____
_____
_____
_____
_____
_____
_____

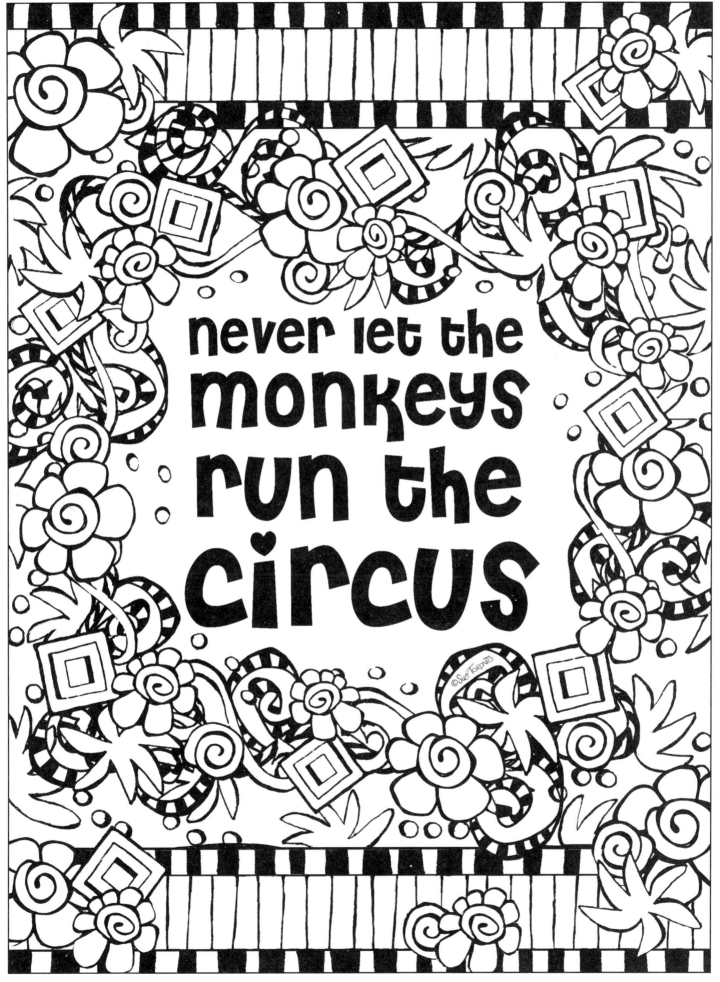

never let the monkeys run the circus

Will you sink or will you swim?
The choice is yours. You are in
control of your destiny and the
possibilities are endless.

_____
_____
_____
_____
_____
_____
_____
_____
_____
_____

Run the Circus

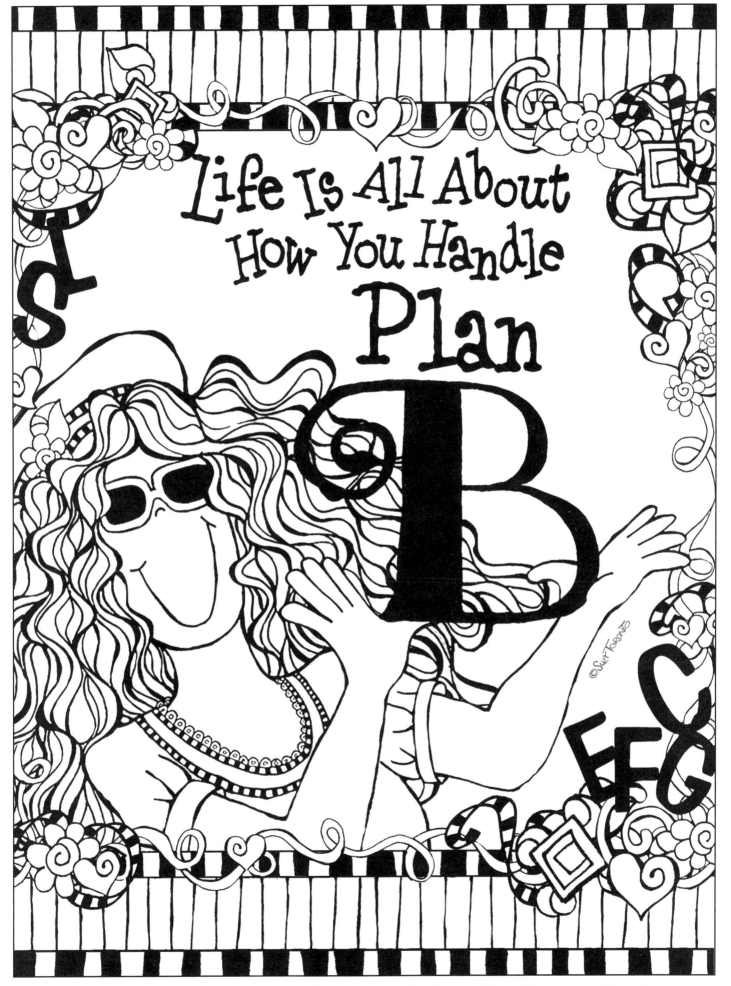

Attitude is the difference between
ordeal and adventure.

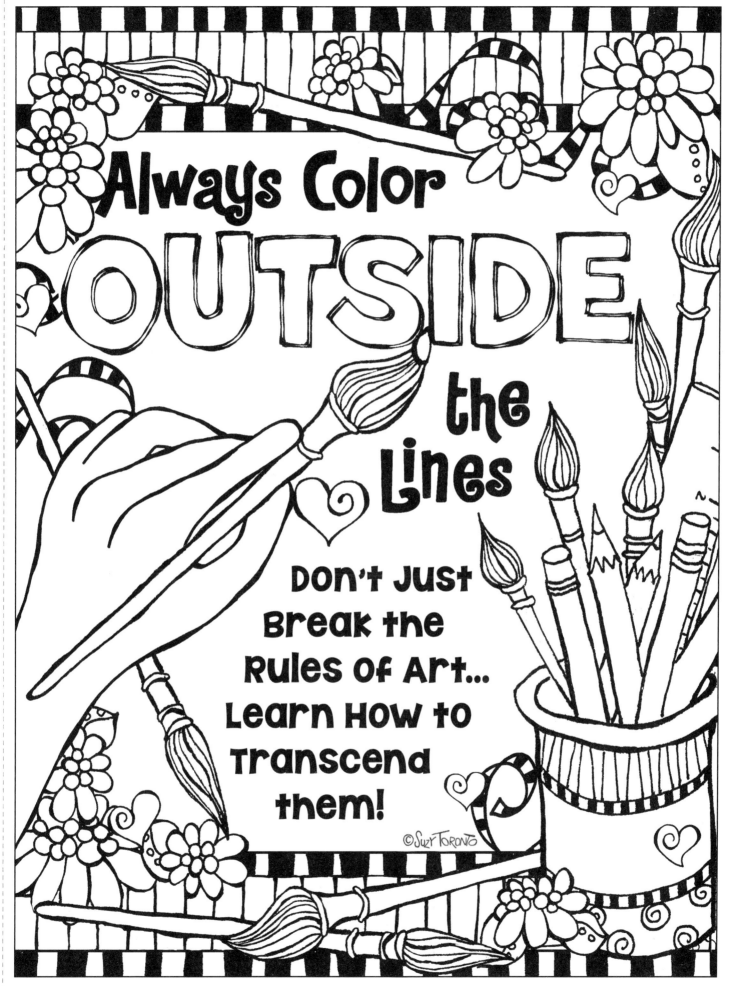

Always Color OUTSIDE the Lines

Don't just break the Rules of Art... Learn How to transcend them!

©Suzy Toronto

Life is a work of heART.
Make yours a masterpiece.

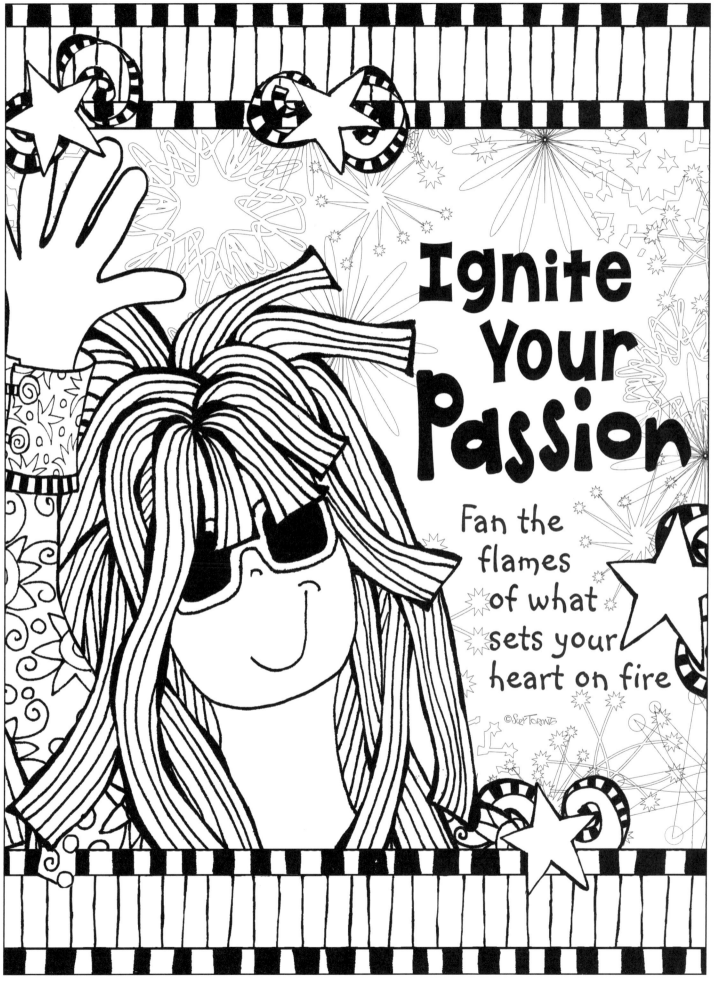

Ignite Your Passion

Fan the flames of what sets your heart on fire

©Suzy Toronto

Do what you love and
live as if that's all there is.

_____
_____
_____
_____
_____
_____
_____
_____
_____

Ignite Your Passion

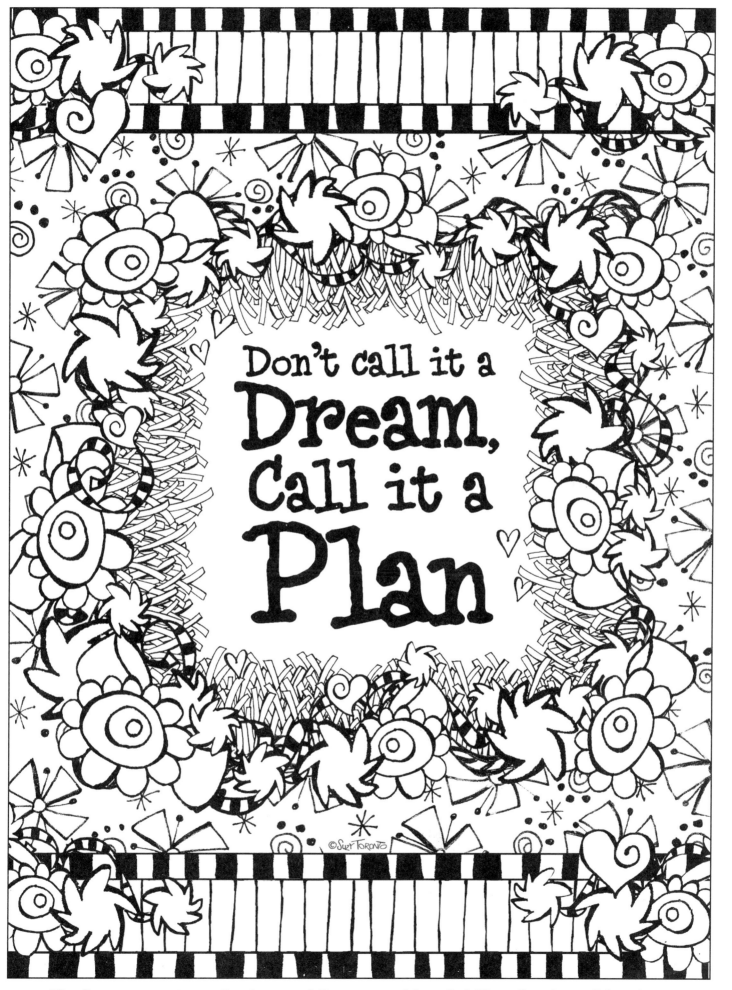

Don't call it a Dream, Call it a Plan

Never say "the sky's the limit."
Live your life without boundaries.

_____
_____
_____
_____
_____
_____
_____
_____
_____
_____

Call It a Plan

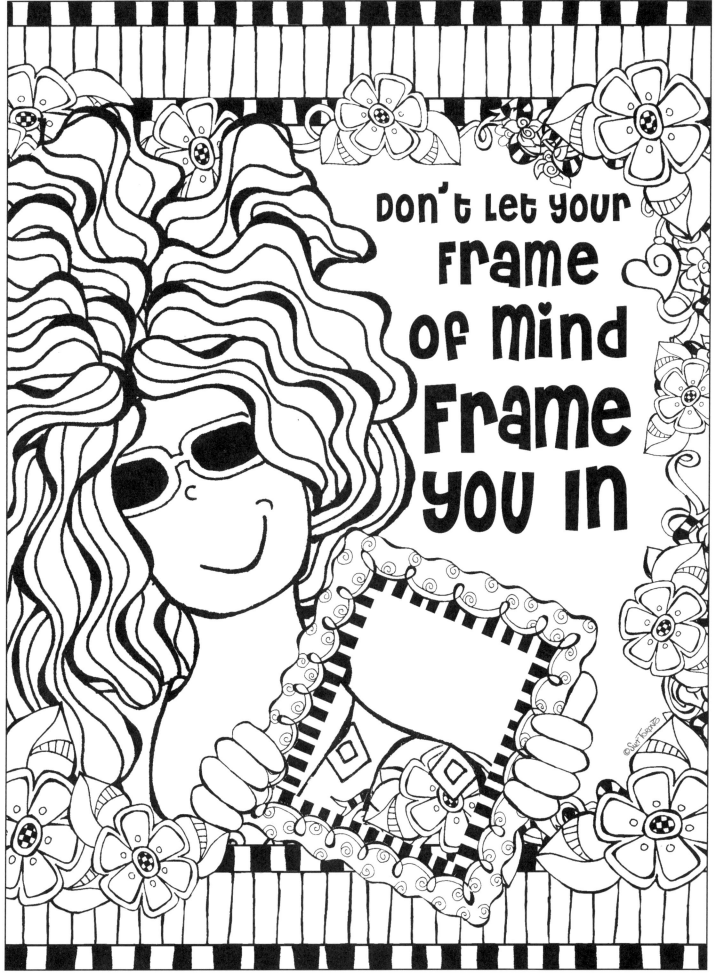

Don't let your frame of mind frame you in

Instead of thinking outside the box,
get rid of the box.

_____
_____
_____
_____
_____
_____
_____
_____
_____

Your Frame of Mind

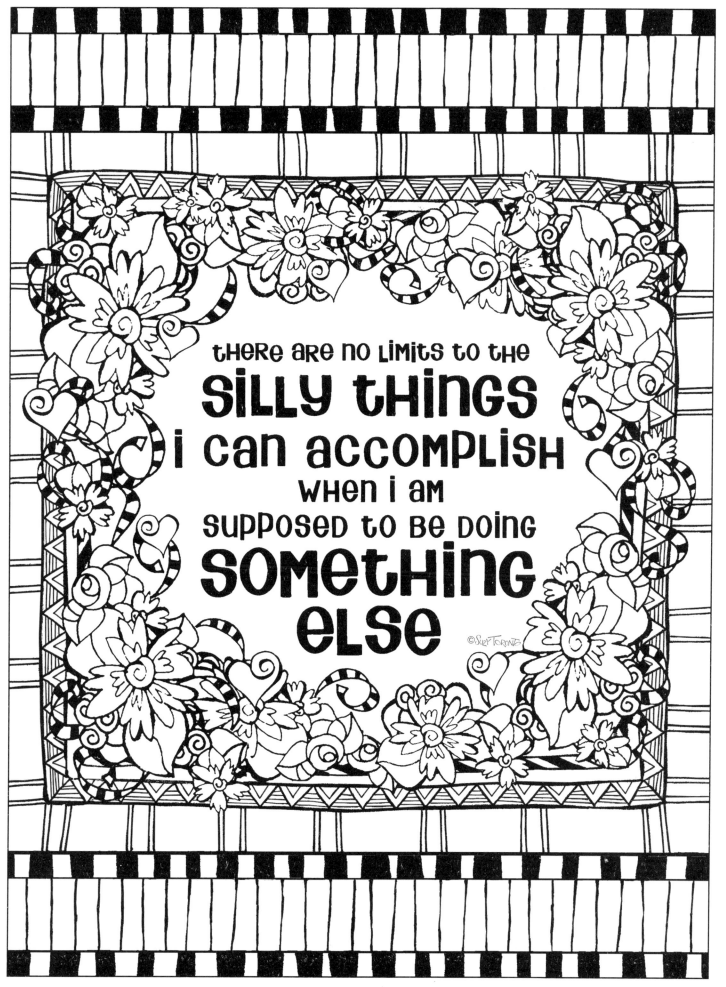

there are no limits to the
SILLY THINGS
i can accomplish
when i am
supposed to be doing
SOMETHING
ELSE

©Suzy Toronto

I meant to be extremely productive today, but there were too many other fun options.

_____
_____
_____
_____
_____
_____
_____
_____
_____
_____

Silly Things

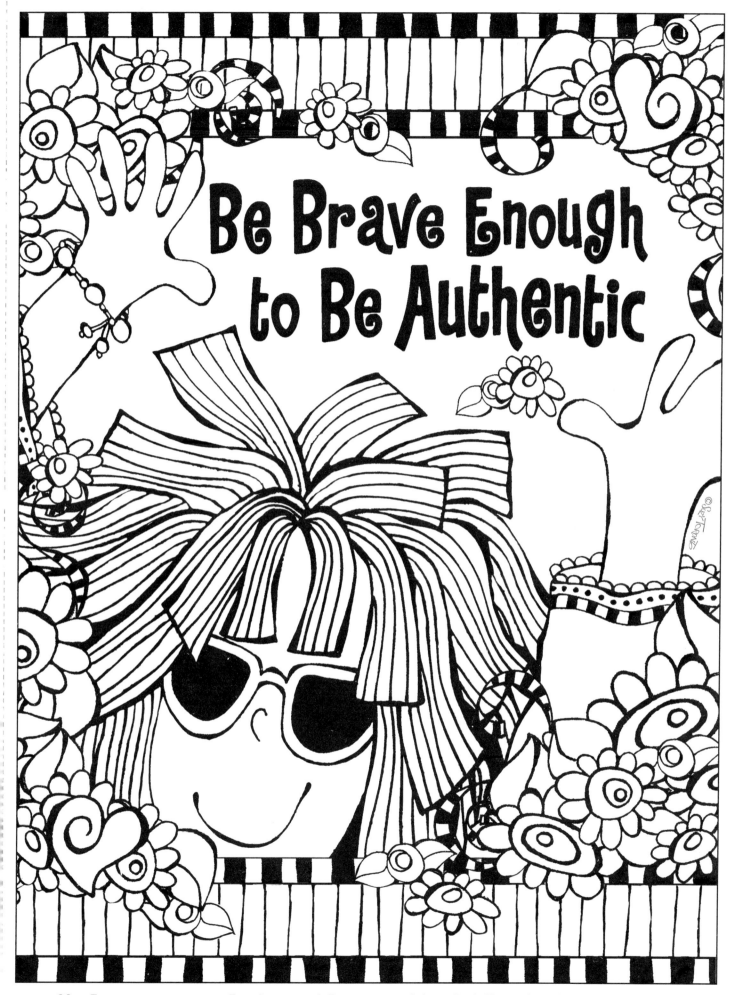

Be yourself—you do NOT have
to act and look like others.

Be Authentic

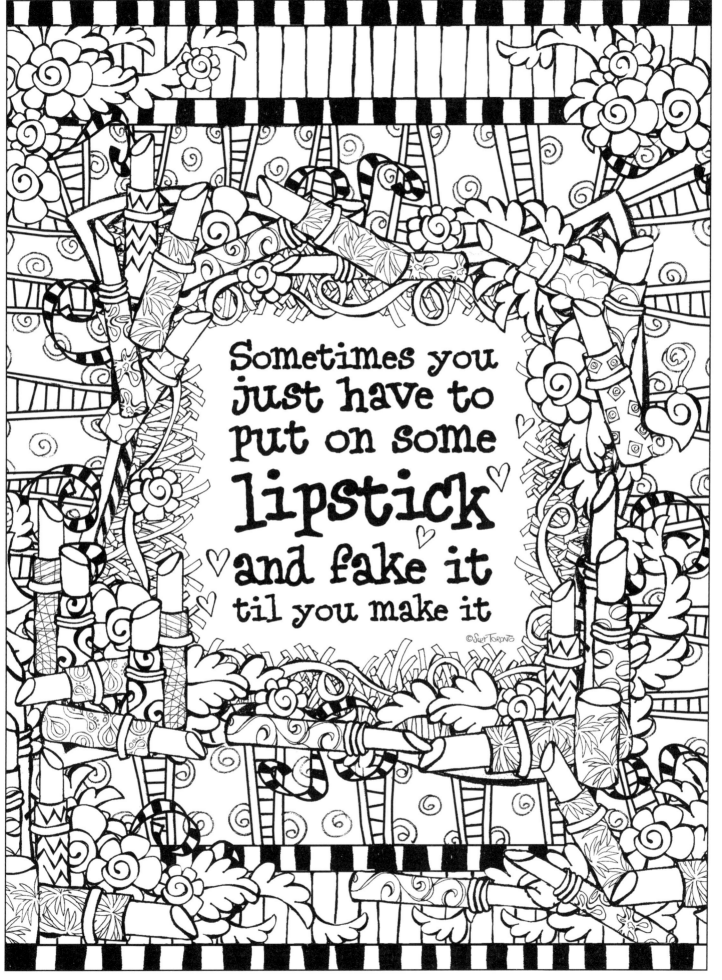

Sometimes you just have to put on some **lipstick** and fake it til you make it

©Suzy Toronto

Some days you just have to act "as if"
every little thing is going to be alright.

_____
_____
_____
_____
_____
_____
_____
_____
_____

Put on Some Lipstick

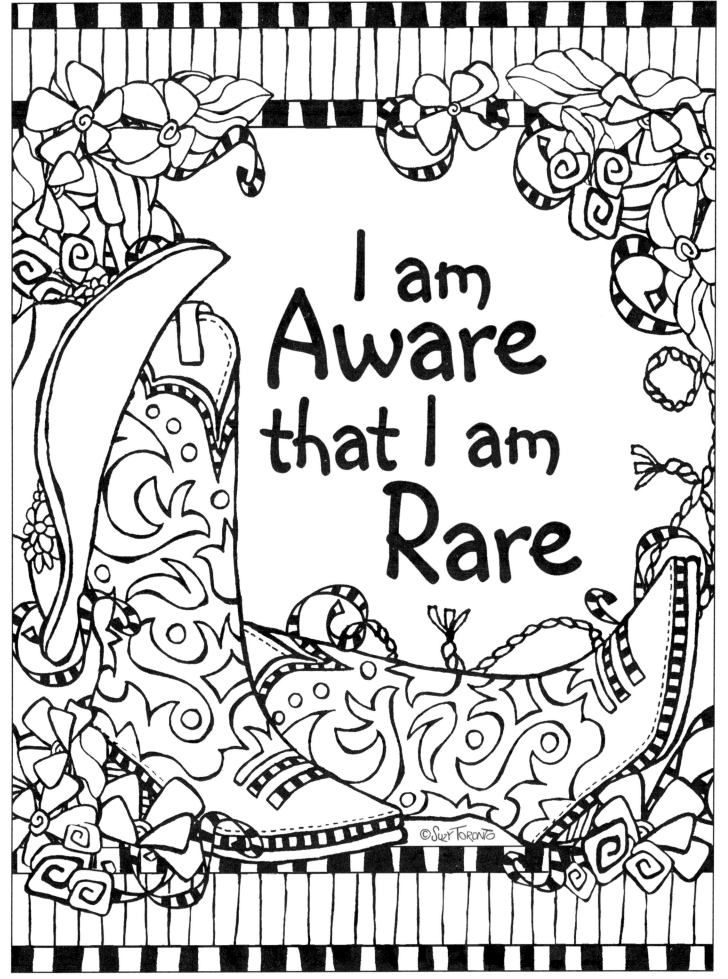

I am
Aware
that I am
Rare

©Suzy Toronto

God doesn't want an orchestra of identical instruments. Why should we all be playing the same tune?

_____
_____
_____
_____
_____
_____
_____
_____
_____

I Am Rare

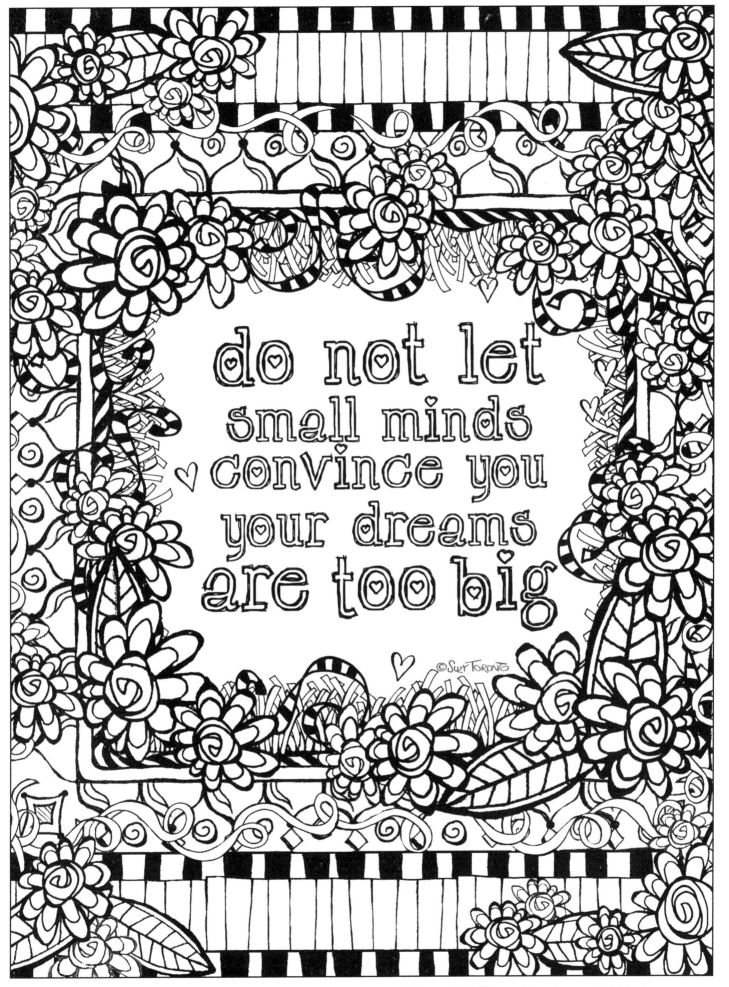

do not let small minds convince you your dreams are too big

©Suzy Toronto

Think big. If that doesn't work,
think bigger. Believe in the
power of your dreams.

_____
_____
_____
_____
_____
_____
_____
_____
_____
_____

Small Minds

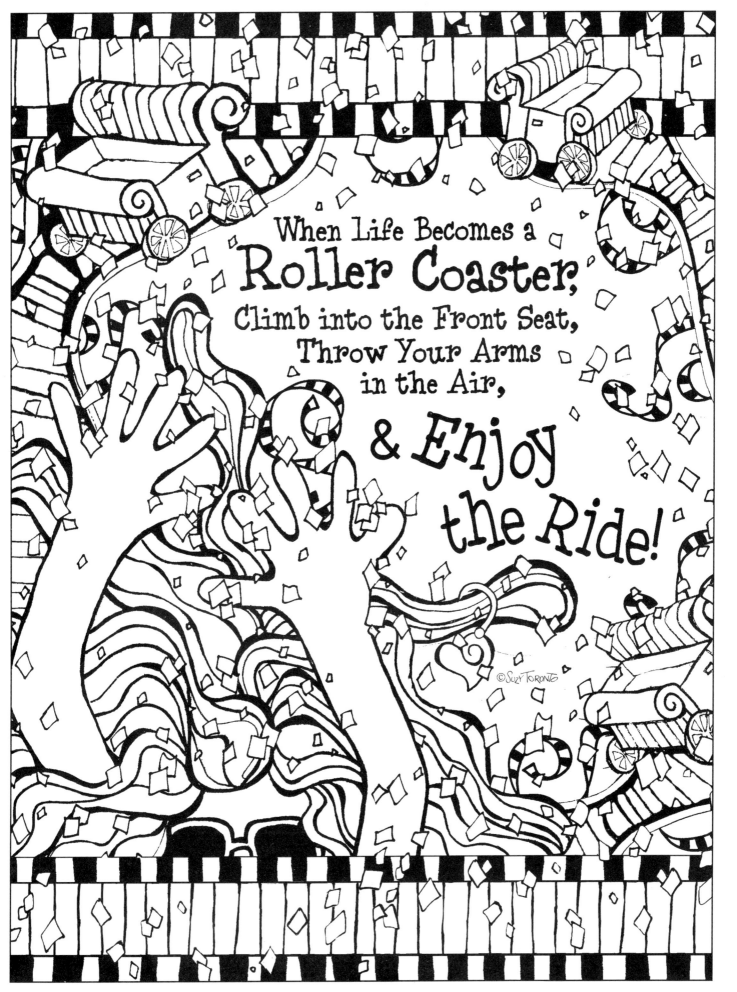

When Life Becomes a **Roller Coaster,** Climb into the Front Seat, Throw Your Arms in the Air, **& Enjoy the Ride!**

©Suzy Toronto

Circumstances don't define us—it's
how we cope with them that does.

_____
_____
_____
_____
_____
_____
_____
_____
_____
_____
_____

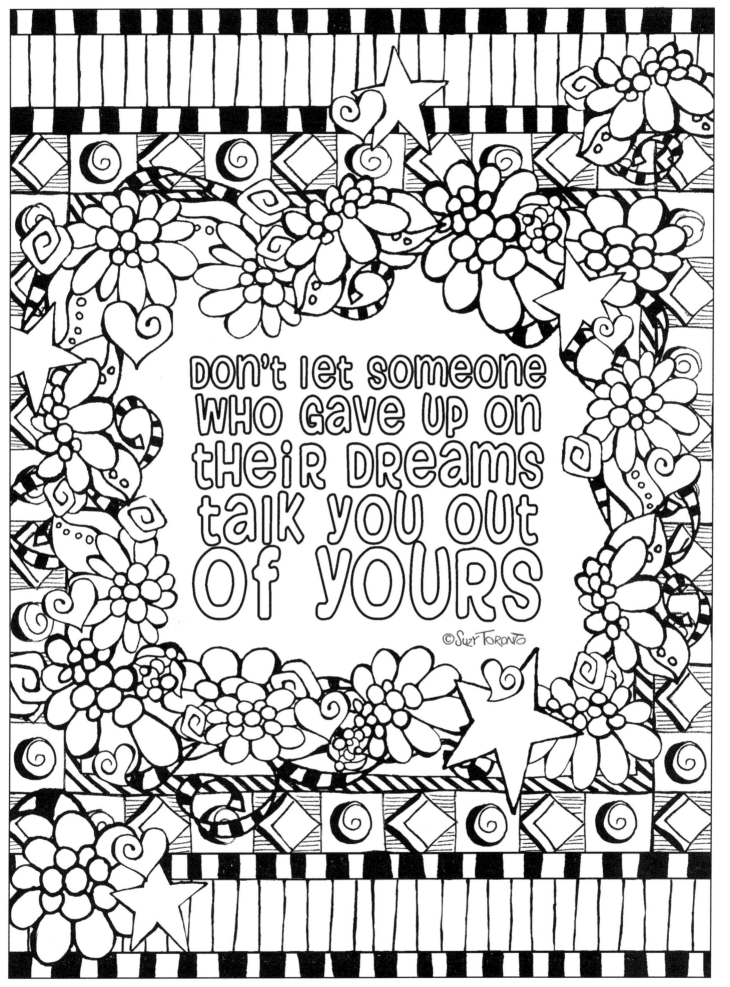

Don't let someone who gave up on their dreams talk you out of YOURS

©Suzy Toronto

Don't live a life of would've,
should've, and could've.

_____
_____
_____
_____
_____
_____
_____
_____

Your Dreams

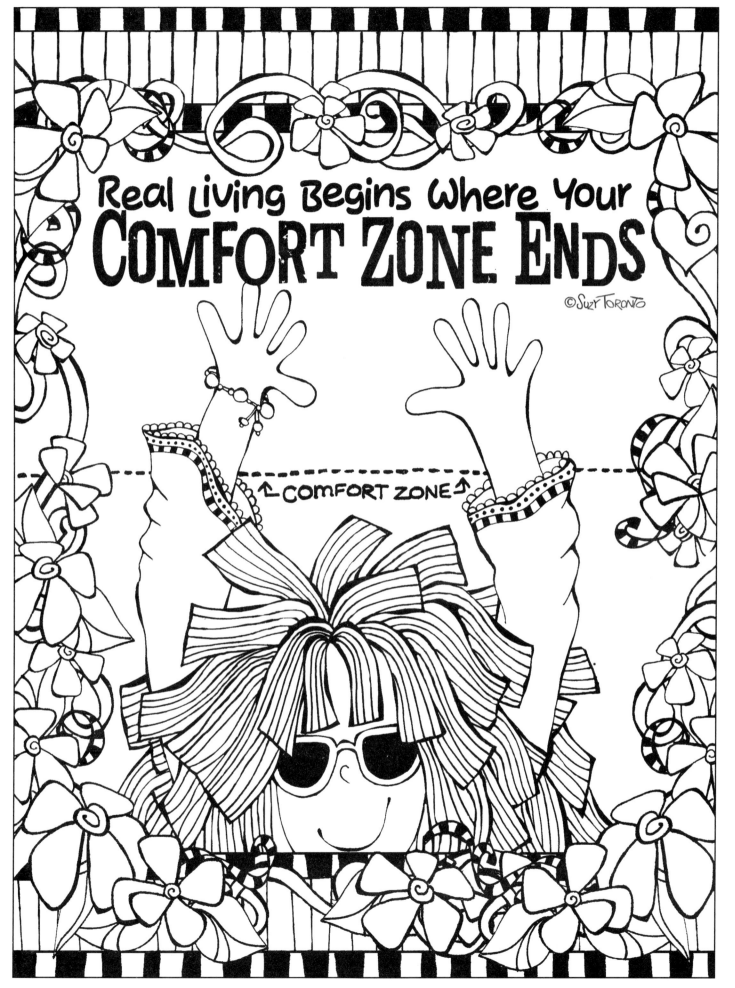

Reach outside your comfort zone.
One of these days, you'll make it.

Your Comfort Zone